Radio Waves for the Blind

Radio Waves for the Blind

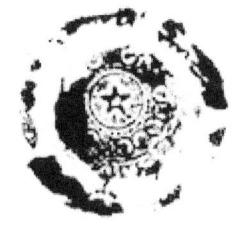

M. D. Veritas

Bon Ton Republic Publications * New Orleans 2019

The new edition is certainly gorgeous — with all the illustrations. I started on
your appendix and am impressed with the huge amount of research and study
you have accomplished. An incredible overview of references. And I believe that
Clare Asquith is mentioned in today's NY Times book review for further work
on Shakespeare. I am indeed honored to receive this extraordinary work; I hope
it will be publicized for its uniqueness and erudition! It should be awarded a
major announcement in libraries everywhere!
Thank you, once again for this thrilling gift!
Best wishes,
Lin

Lin Emery   Nov 25, 2018, from an email concerning new Shakespeare AI trilogy vols.

Part IV, Shakespeare AI: Soul of the Iconcurchaic Age, a Quadrilogy

Numbers in brackets beside titles are Shakespeare Sonnet numbers for allusions
in each line of the poem shown in italics.

ISBN: 978-1-7328146-4-6
Bon Ton Republic Publications, All Rights Reserved
mdveritas52@gmail.com

LUX ET VERITAS

To the memories of Guy Charleville, Susan Austell,

Vivian Moncrief, Maxine Cassin, Phyllis Hudson

& Henry Ross

For Janice, Diana & Lin

Behold, Thou desirest truth in the inward parts:

and in the secret part Thou shalt make me to know wisdom.

To the chief musician: a Psalm of David (51)

Blind loving wrestling touch, sheath'd hooded sharp-tooth'd touch!
Did it make you ache so, leaving me?

Walt Whitman, *Leaves of Grass*

Science without religion is lame; religion without science is blind.

Albert Einstein

Woe to you, you impious scribes and Pharisees! you traverse sea and land to make a single proselyte, and when you succeed, you make him a son of Gehenna twice as bad as yourselves. Woe to you, blind guides that you are! you say, "Swear by the sanctuary, and it means nothing; but swear by the gold of the sanctuary, and the oath is binding." You are senseless and blind! for which is the greater, the gold or the sanctuary that makes the gold sacred?

Matthew 23:15-17 (James Moffatt, Trans.)

That the green leaves came and covered the high rock,
That the lilacs came and bloomed, like a blindness cleaned,
Exclaiming bright sight, as it was satisfied,

In birth of sight.

Wallace Stevens, *The Rock*

Contents

I. Blind Hindsight
Going West to Go East   3
To Helgoland and Back   4
Würzburg / Warsburg: Still-Film   6
The New World Order Big Mac Attack   9
Obama of Arabia Wish List   10
Finishing Touches on the Broken Obelisk   11
Three Biblical Resurrections   12
Bible Salesman, Florence, South Carolina, 1971   13
Panamanian Manmade Void, 1974   18
Rest and Reflection on Fern Street, 1981   22
Dreaming of the Murdered Coed Together, 1991   24
Improvising Redemption   25
Lunar Teacher Eclipse, 1992   27
Multiple Places on the Lost Highway Stops Here   28
The Wave-Bell Invocation, 1981   29
Isaiah's Inspiration   31
Touching on Rowena's Return, 1991   33
Special Agents   35
Reluctant Patron   37
Inexhaustible Wine   39
Building Trade's Ars Poetica   41
La Belle Orleanna of the Wetlands   42
The Missing Song Redux, 2005   45

II. Romantique Fantasia
Luxury Limbo Hotel   49
The Whirlwind Sessions   50
The Non-Writing Writer's One-Prong Recovery Crown   51
    1) Asleep on the Ethernet
    2) To Define or not to Define
    3) Mystery Book Horse Ride
    4) The Lost Generation Reformed
    5) Politics of Seduction
    6) Her 12 String Program
    7) To Write or not to Write
The Whirlwind Sessions II   58
Subway to Cezanne's Rainbow   60

III. Big Bang Nutshell Time's Haunted Generation
Visionary Angelic Visitation   65
Blinded Sight to See   66
Resurrection Epiphany   67
Haunted Generation   70
Monumental Proposal   71
Recycling Lee Circle   72
Ai Weiwei at Home   73
World War III Museum   74
Swimming with the Great White Whale   75
Big Bang Nutshell Time   78
  1) Stephan Hawking's M-Theory of Everything
  2) Redundant Pyramids: Cydonia / Cairo
  3) Galactic Origami Soul
Lux Volupté's Calm Matisse Harbor   81
Mother's Spirit   82
A Sect of One (Plus One)   83
Haunted Generation 2   85
  1) Quantum Entanglement
  2) Heavenly Dream World: First Level
  3) Her Next Life Visitation
Yeats' Last Paradigm Vision   88
Her Unburdened Prescience   89
Lin Emery Circle's Cursive Flight   90
Hunched over Notre Dame   91
Celestial Accounting with Cubits   92
Delicate Thunder Embraced Awareness   93
Apocalyptic Cycle   94
Guy's Revivified Mind   95
Credit where Credit's Due   96
Angel Trumpets   97
  1) All for your Everything
  2) Time Heals, Wounds to Heal
  3) Spirit Guide
  4) Incarnadine Mind
  5) Divined Family
  6) Great Catch
  7) Body's Heir
ASAP: Age of Second Adam's Paradigm   104
Under the Orbital Lilac Tree   105
A Unified Field Ballad   106

Appendix

Fields of Dreams: Symbols of Consciousness 109

Acknowledgments 124

Illustrations (in order):

Susan & I

Portrait of M. D. Veritas

Lin Emery's *Flight* as Various Angel Wings

Hamlet's Seal 1604

Lin's *Flight* Rising from the Underworld with Orpheus

Angel with Spiritual Sun

Orpheus Rising with Lin's *Flight* Waves

Grasping the Unattainable

Cezanne's Mardi Gras Studio

Night Trolley to the Afterlife with Lin's *Flight*

Angel's Reach from Shadows

Atomic Head for Winged Nike Forming (thanks to Salvador Dali)

Particle Collision, crop 3

Painterly Cloud 1

Contrail Cross over Flashing Angel with Broken Wing

I. Blind Hindsight

Going West to go East

One night to next,
moon parts sky
1/20th inch per second
to bottomless sarcophagus.

Observing shadows on the moon,
Aristotle saw skull curves
& knew earth was round.
We no longer need
Brunelleschi's mirror perspective
when eyes travel circles
to center the universe.
As Toscanelli bent his map grid
into a cylinder the first time,
sailors barged into a new world,
sailing west to Chippangu
in the Far East.

A powder burned moon arcs heights,
Newton's cannon shot off the sun's
invisibly tethered twin poles,
a cloudless dusted form of first stones,
one-sided pull exposed no spin
above a school of diving dolphins
leaping tranquilities of their own,
hunched to tides pulling their weight home.

Rounding out universe comprehension,
had Einstein counting universal dice
he threw incomprehensively magnetized,
summed up what makes it comprehensible,
eclipsing sun for moon's bent shadows,
equating star points behind the sun,
dark optic balance measured swerves
ellipse orbits in a gridlocked world,
as gravity's new moon recycles light
slung from the western sun rising east.

To Helgoland and Back

1
Ledged on the North Sea, a mind wanders
foothills of Mars or Saturn's crashed asteroid,
when red cliffs of Helgoland appear
to anchor the world's widest beach at ebb tide.
Silt shimmers in heavy water that sifts
gold filament deposits, perpetual night
of every dead creature & plant churned up
& pulverized by the wheeling waters.

Surf pounds the high seas side, cliffs like ruins
of some antediluvian kingdom fortress
that echoed power from times of Norsemen rites
to Nazi submarine pins in hollowed caves
the British bombed even after the war
for target practice alerting future blitzkriegers
who'll fall like lightning off cliffs of delirium
where Helgoland warns like uncured radium.

2
First week of June on Cuxhaven beach
looking out to Helgoland cliffs,
serene Vivian Moncrief sat with me,
a strawberry cheeked blonde beauty
in a yellow wicker beach shell's
Bremerhaven High School picnic.
We spoke briefly of college plans,
she wanted love in love with knowledge.

She asked to remove her blouse,
I did not object or blush,
"You're not like other boys," she remarked
white bra pointing to cliff-hanging red
In one final Bremerhaven summer,
walking far from friends to check courage,
charge their memories & my memory of them,
I walked to where tides trawl wonder's edge.

4

With horizontal gravity Helgoland swells
on the horizon as silt soft sand withdraws,
tide suctioned evenly under advancing feet.
Five miles out water laps shins to knees
on the lip edge of a swallowing North Sea.
A kilometer after rubber-capped bathers,
in lawn chairs under umbrellas, read papers,
before wind blows wave-caps white & back
the diagonal ledge of shelf appears.
On the left its sand-wedge curves to Helgoland,
at right a starboard freighter steers to port.

Into toe-curled brine, seven sinking steps
to trudge across the waters chopping block,
no murk of half-ground fish bones, shells & kelp,
then kick & crawl over the table top
where waves yawn chilled swells of deeper sea.
Embracing sways afloat before a dive
to peering prayer through blurred stings of salt,
sun shafts flare like mid-day train lights on track
to disappearing tunnels for nowhere,
then breaking surface to find Helgoland
a mirage throb on foreshortened horizon.

3
Ten years later waking half inflamed,
wet from a dream, surf pulsing the brain,
the body hot in conch shell spiral brine,
mouth fishy from outgoing tide…

a tropical afternoon New Orleans June rain,
clutching the pillow like Vivian's waist
at Bremerhaven's prom on the dance floor,
then with her alone in the beach shell,
recalled sensation of bare feet in sand
a slight parting kiss, a touch of her hand,
on Cuxhaven beach, back to Helgoland.

epilogue:
Twenty-four years from Bremerhaven a friend called,
said Vivian died by murder or suicide
around '92, when this poem was first published
at the University of New Orleans.

5

Würzburg / Warsburg: Still Film

He... delivered... his glory to the hand of the foe. –Psalm 78:61

"60,000,000 francs for an occupation that may not last a day.
The sale assures forever the power of the United States
and I have given England a rival who... will humble her pride."
–Napoleon on selling Louisiana to Jefferson

Mixing victor & vanquished, stirring new blood,
Würzburg bred me to bear its artistic flood,
into the new world after childhood looking up,
poured baroque allegory in my loving cup.

As Bishop's seat gridded on a Catholic chess map,
Würzburg received Napoleon's visit trap,
who quartered himself at the "Residenz,"
praised the bishop for its Versailles influence,

admired Tiepolo's "Myth of America,"
from Balthasar Neumann's five-bayed staircase.
He scanned the upper story gallery vista,
spanned unsupported single canopied vault face,

white lofting panoramic billowed frozen sails,
Antonio Bossi's stucco draperied plot,
Tiepolo's operatic fresco councils,
continents under Apollo's sun chariot

rising through the gold tinged upper abyss spire
from four quarters of the globe below Olympus
accompanied by muses with lyre & choir,
bright heralds of his musical appearance.

On terraced clouds chariot & sun-steeds arrive,
the hours harness & mark the zodiacs wheel,
Autumn, Bacchus of seasons, Mars & Venus live
at leisure, heavy clouds loom their perches sequel

6

in nether regions, unknown American gloom
where stucco giants shape a dreamy Greek vision
halfway edged between the scene & the room,
turned within to break the onlooker's framed caution.

Beneath dark clouds America's queen Indian
in black, blue, red feathered headdress, bow on shoulder,
jeweled necklace, earrings of gold & medallion,
points from a tapestry saddled alligator

surrounded by her retinue of followers
to bear their gifts to the great civilization
of Europeans who built these decked out wonders
under the banner of von Greiffenclau's union.

Winged lizard, shares their feathered drum beat festivals,
with severed heads, alligator meat collections,
her silver sun-calendar gift of survivals,
peace making coffee, cocoa drink-tray confections,

while others roast meat on an open-flamed spit,
sweet maiden head-totes a wine pot to feast
spied by the painter on his knees from a pit,
behind a canvas he hides from the rest.

The other half gathers with Europa,
globe beside her throne, listening to musicals,
Holy Roman banners blow by Barbarossa
with portraits of artists & notables.

Hildebrandt said he'd hang himself if the vault held,
Neumann offered to fire artillery below.
Bossi died insane but his stucco never failed
even when Allied bombs laid the cathedral low.

The Residenz survived like a miracle save,
ninety percent of the town in a grave,
the world's widest mural lived out heaven's concern,
prevailed to show who'd destroy, rebuild the nation.

A psychic still-film unfolds from myth to future,
the storied past restored in paint & plaster,
perpetually processed *now* through disaster,
the eyes of her child returned as art master.

Radio Luxemburg contemplated the state
of Europe's ten-horned head, on seven headed beast,
NATO's Star Wars Council as Würzburg's destined fate,
emerged to converge through clouds & veiled paint to feast

on crumbled Colossus feet of iron & clay clod,
The Holy Roman Empire's last resurrection,
not Nebuchadnezzar's shattered dream's cosmic rod,
shattered by the rock hewn & hurled by no human,

the ripened rock growing the Kingdom of God,
hurled from the *Book of Daniel* to *Revelation*,
awakened to catastrophe in lands of Nod,
from Newton to Einstein's double gravitation.

When bombers dropped apocalyptic pyres,
perfected ash & rubble of war fires,
on paper Würzburg made of living words,
created my birth flight from a home for the birds,

to crack the orbital code of the lilac tree,
the vessels of old town's broken burned mystery,
renewed from incognito, revelation's piece,
composed a second coming to come in peace.

for Sandra Baker

The New World Order's Big Mac Attack

The under arm of a dismantled Lenin
blocked the entrance to McDonald's in Red Square
where Marx godfathered, would never miss a meal
though a combo once cost about two weeks wages
& fast food lines lurch lunches hours long.

His glowing body, surfaced to be removed
after decades rivaling mummified pharaohs,
from the aquarium in Red Square,
Lenin's pickled brain was taken to room 16,
diced condiments from the Ministry of Mysteries.

In 1991 the "Fail-Safe" bombers
disarmed for the first time in 34 years,
as if a dying wish of Armand Hammer,
the only western business man Lenin trusted,
desperate for post-revolution baking soda.

Wyoming Senator Wallop's memoriam,
the lone "Strangelove" dissention ranger to disarm
START II nuclear cuts, now wins trumped to rearm,
flies Götterdämmerung far through fahrvergnügen,
passed golden arched embassy, Jerusalem.

in memory of James Tate

Obama of Arabia Wish List

Ring welcome bells for workers homeless in fruit fields,
ring Bernie's welcome, teachers, libertarians,
ring bells for citizens who lost how freedom feels,
ring bells Syrian committed Europeans
who once pursued Obama of Arabia
to cut the seasoned rosebuds of Arcadia,
fly them over busy middle eastern seas,
airlifted for beach combing refugees,
who left all behind to dine on Europe's grass
till peace season grows as fast as more will pass.
New Syrians maneuver, Corfu gets through Greece,
with nothing left to lose, only the barren fleece,
imagine NATO drones escaping Crimea,
new Russian Republics of Academia.

Finishing Touches on the Broken Obelisk

Torn from its roots in Karnak, Washington,
a fractured wisdom tooth of martyrdom,
inverted pyramid pinnacle's undone points
to bond the capstone of pyramid conundrum,
achieves more in deserts than suburban haunts.

This broken obelisk anchors Rothko's chapel
to Houston's sky, Martin Luther King's memory.
Raw rust black brown on the dreamer's stagnation pool,
reflected KKK, swastika graffiti,
the touched up chalk scrawl, a death-marks hollow pity.

In Rothko's vaulted icons sacrifice stands trial,
a cut out tongue vast as light behind emptiness,
a mess of muddy blood flow's silhouetted Nile
drought citizenship of soul through murk to confess
the cross & spear of destiny's stone-hearted kindness.

The painter stood at canvas wall, reflected back
to face its mirror stone with brush & razor sights,
blurred portrait smeared, a self-portrayed Christ-hack.
A Judas kissed executioner's last hung rights,
achieved what dried blood does in dimming chapel lights.

Three Biblical Resurrections

*

You know you will go into light,
    not how, when, momentarily
you will see love's expectant ones
    return from where they ascended
through the clouds with his retinue,
    among those of whom you're numbered.

*

Sun melts to obsidian ash
    in sleep so deep no time has passed,
dead a day or six thousand years.
    The roll of an eye awakens
from a multitude of dry bones,
    fleshed out and catching re-skinned breath,
questioning a final event,
    wondering about last judgment,
majesty of renewed world,
    rebuilt a thousand years by them
with those who resurrected first,
    those reborn in that quantum time.

*

A huge fire-lake burns like sun
    across a great expanse of space,
a chance to accept the kingdom
    after second resurrection
given but rather be going
    to wherever they'll know nothing
& those that knew them will not know
    they forgot them, who had to go.

Bible Salesman's Progress (University of Wyoming, 1971)

-a freshman's first journey from home

1

The view of Snowy Ridge from the tenth floor
of McIntyre Hall in Laramie,
held peaceful contemplated suicides
for freshmen who could not commune with saints,
returning lost expatriated souls.

No evangelical night clerk would wait
before giving flight in the prayer circle,
to demons of lost girlfriend drunk despair,
when catching the determined sobbing freshman,
one floor ahead in elevator chase.

The out-of-breath golden-curled Jesus clerk
with snow-burned, apple-cheek angel-faced smile,
inquired of dazed freshmen at hall breakfast
& found the tactful way to counseling
while winning over other souls for Christ.

New friends would show up at the evening prayers.
Group gathered drives to Garden of the Gods,
retreat with elders sharing their rich Bibles,
skilled in fine points of subtle cross translation
for meanings & discerning spirit vibes,

surmising books, *The Late Great Planet Earth*.
They planned attending *Jesus Christ Superstar*,
discussing how it made Jesus look lost.
At year's end summer jobs would reappear
for selling Bibles from the Tennessee sales school.

They say the Jesus clerk made 8,000
in cash after Nashville classes last year
by selling in Florence, South Carolina.
The freshman passed, sees himself on the road
determined to make a killing through Christ.

2

The clerk's young brother once lost then signed up,
when grades were posted the three drove away.
The shiny new Volkswagon Beetle filled
with cases of all things that they would need
without the Jesus clerk who'd meet them there.

Somewhere in Colorado the pre-salesman
sits in the backseat between suitcases,
they groove Led Zeppelin loud on the 8-track.
The other two get stoned & joke, he nods out
then suddenly jumps from a dream of driving

off some dark stormy cliff with screaming friends.
Relived to find it just a dream, they laugh.
The next bright morning our ex-freshman jolts
from two quick hammer blows upon his crown,
awake eyes glare at a world upside down.

He saw in sleep the first blow as a dream,
the second opened his eyes to the light,
a dirt spray filled them feeling like water.
The beetle rolled back on its wheels & went
downhill at ditch & fence, turned, rolled again.

They rolled through Nashville in a new Toyota
& went to Bible sales school for a week,
then filled the car with Bibles & drove out
for Florence, South Carolina to sell,
rented a boarding room on the edge of town.

3

First morning the salesmen start out early,
he's dropped off at city limits & walks
the outer county with his sample case.
He wears a tie, white shirt, dark suit, new shoes,
rehearses lines to yield many orders.

If you're unhappy, return the Bibles
& we will refund your purchase soon in full,
you will have thirty days free to enjoy them.
Your orders may be placed in small down payments,
& yes, we will most gladly accept your check.

He does not stop at the first house he sees,
not wanting to come on as over eager,
so he waits for the last house in the row.
No one comes to the door, he leaves relieved
back to the asphalt, to sweat by the fields.

He passed a close Black man who plowed with mules,
thick pines, then on a road bent to few houses.
A mother invites him in her small house,
with samples he tries to speak over three kids,
they cry & she can't buy a Bible right now.

Across the street a young woman hangs clothes,
her lovely smile surprises as she says hi.
At ease by her big yard, large house on a rise,
he speaks of how his first day started out,
she brings him in for water & grandmother,

retired teacher, a Bible scholar.
She listens seriously with pleasure,
asks if he knows the King James & Jesus.
He tells how his conversion brought the job,
convinced he's saved, her check's for a concordance.

4
Into the long driveway of a rich farmer,
they offer milk & wafers listening
to his sales pitch as lunchtime entertainment,
until they get their laugh & send him packing
with ribbing for this hard work in his life.

He took a dirt road by a burned out shell
& stopped at chimney ruins for a break.
A tractor drove up with two men to load
parts of house rubble on a pulled wagon.
The driver greets him friendly with small talk.

The startled salesman smiles, explains his presence,
how first he sold a book then was turned away
by rich folk who had Bibles, wanted laughs.
The man then understood & introduced
himself & his friend, Amos he, and Randy.

Amos wants to know about the Bibles,
says he'd buy one gladly but can't read,
although his daughter in Nashville needs one.
Randy, who had a stroke, drinks a lot,
can't use books either, they help each other out.

The salesman thanks him for encouragement,
accepts a ride to a country crossroads store.
Inside he buys some chips & a cold drink,
the store man sees his case, asks for a pitch,
but it's too hard to sell Bibles too refreshed.

5
A piece of walk away stood some small shacks.
A young Black woman on a front porch sat,
kindly listened then invited him in
to grandma at her sitting room backdoor
who apologized for her leprosy.

She said sunlight was bad for her skin
& wanted to hear about the books again,
the Bible gave her all her pleasure now;
she'd half the cost saved for the big print book,
he wanted to take off the other half.

He could not ask the poor to buy Bibles.
One last brick house landlord to turn him down,
as dark came he looked for a place to lay
just off the road, maybe under a tree,
then noticed the lit bulb on a shack porch.

Out stepped Amos & Randy smiling a wave,
delighted to share their egg shrimp panned rice.
When offered sleep, a mattress & clean sheet,
the kindness felt a deeper sense of peace,
than selling Bibles had of unseen rewards.

The next day Amos gave him directions
that proved he returned the county's full circle.
An hour later at the boarding house
he saw the car repacked with Bibles
& entered the room where his friends wondered

if he had sales & where he'd spent the night.
He told them, asked about the refilled car.
The driver said he drove to town & joined
the Navy & must now prepare for war
which sold the salesman's case to a carpenter's helper.

for Paul Cutting

Panamanian Manmade Void (1974 - 99)

I
At sunset jungle birds stop screeching
when thousands of bats stream from river caves,
behind vines, cocobolo trees & bush,
the rainy season on Rio Baho.

Strumming Neil Young's "Down by the River,"
in Levi cut-offs on a Martin guitar,
shin-high in the river, bats flapping by,
strobbing twilight into dizzy bat-river sky,

voice tuned into a liquid tremolo,
"She-ee-naa, dra-ag me-ee o-ovaa, the ra-ainbo-ow…"
bat sonar pinging off every sharp "E-O,"
close up bat faces flash in the blinking solo.

The first night medics listened from tent cots
as monkeys shriek greetings, shake perimeter trees.
New morning's villagers fill treatment tents,
afternoon clockwork rain drenches everything.

Ills range from lockjaw to elephantiasis.
General Torreos relocates natives,
indigenous tribes to the interior,
to complete the dam at Columbia's border.

Last link of Pan-American highway,
Alaska through Chile, stands back from the river,
awaiting water eighty feet high,
enough hydro-power to light this sky.

The day our deuce-and-a-halves forded the river
with jeeps & gamma-goats, a worker fell 80 feet,
got choppered to Panama City,
in what took trucks eight hours, in 20 minutes.

For millennia Indians pole-walked canoes
loaded with bananas, melons & fish,
passed wives in dyed sarongs & gold neck rings,
standing in pairs on the banks to wave & watch.

Canoes round the bend with a standing brave
echoing chants like neighbor conductors to tribes,
gliding by thousands of round rocks,
the last day I collected flecks of gold from rocks broke.

II
On jungle-base hill, Ft. Gulick, Canal Zone,
a rainy night radio crackled, a ranger
ran into black palm, needed a medic.
I stormed off the hilltop from our circle

barreling down a bush tunnel road,
lights bounce off rain like television snow,
hit dips in the road, wheels lock to skid,
a sideways glide into bush slump,

headlight silhouettes bush branched windshield,
thrown four-wheel-drive gunned reverse just spins,
the goat jerks down a few vibrating feet,
swaying in the diesel drone behind the seat.

Cut power, wonder about the ditch,
recall repelling & Cliff Evac class,
only now I'd be the man on my back
pulled up through the window frame to push off.

Turn to the cab, step up the wheel-well,
feel for the trailer canopy drip-edge,
lean in slide-stepping the trailer ledge
to the tailgate back & break in the bush,

jump to full moon rain road, race the rain back.
Another goat goes for the injured ranger.

Three of us wait in the back of a goat
on cots smoke joints & joke about the load.

We laugh recalling Larry Chance & the panther
walking by his goat as he pisses in the bush.
We crack up at the look on his face when
a six inch spider breaks the surgical light circle

at our eye-trained feet we seize, jump & shriek,
spill coke & beer, cigarettes and joints,
my leg cocks an automatic soccer shot
& kicks the spider through the tailgate goal.

The next bright morning a wrecker driver motions,
smiling beside the stuck goat, to walk up,
& pulls back the bush to an eighty foot drop,
bucolic waterfalls stream rocks in a clearing.

III
On a hill across from Contractor's Hill,
300 foot cliffs line, each side, leaned back
where the canal looks sliced through a layer cake
iced by thousands who died from yellow fever,

Pip and I on a noon ambulance call,
reading & strumming in our gamma goat,
wait for injured G.I.s playing war.
We sit & lie in the canopy shade.

As I lean over the tailgate, look at the sky,
a half circle glows, a rainbow of gold,
like Frederic Church's waterfall rainbows
painted from excursions to the tropics.

I stretch out further to see where it goes,
in disbelief it's unbroken, complete!
The circle halos the sun-centered sky
& sets off the sky in two tones of blue!

The deeper blue within the inner edge
bends the path of small clouds like a lens.
The lighter blue outside makes the rainbow
a sky-hole to an unsearchable light.

I shouted the natural world's epiphany,
Pip just read, waiting to go home & said,
"Oh yeah, I saw the rainbow, it was neat,
around the sun like it made a big eye."

IV
Struck by a dry open-field late twilight,
not far from certain peaks of Darien
where star-tossed skies swell Panamanian,
I watched three stars arc the dome of the night.

The first flash flared a diamond pin-point bright.
Waiting watch with an ambulance to win
the cause for a soldier to rise again,
a ten times brighter flare streaked the great height.

Surmising near calamity of awe,
I challenged the "Presence" for a third try.
No scientific experimental law
could keep a flash from light-blinding the eye,
out of the shadows a foxbat strafed my flaw,
diving from God's "comet" lit by firefly!

V
A year later I woke up in Würzburg to see
Omar Torreos' wet smile in "The Stars and Stripes,"
after diving into the man-made lake,
from a road atop Rio Baho's dam.

He later died in a mystery plane crash
some blame on sly Noriega's power grab.
Last photo of Torreos with Jimmy Carter,
all smiles signed over the Canal in '99.

for John Constantine

21

Rest and Reflection on Fern Street

A squirrel jumps to pinched rattail stem from frond
to eat sweet flowers of a banana tree pod.
From my deck chair, with pomegranate & pen,
the sun blinks through the backyard canopy garden.

A fresh breeze sighs in New Orleans off Carrollton,
three doors removed from Maple Street & Fern.
A Mozart violin piano diversion
from WTUL wafts to prop feet on.

Below the half-breeze blossomed magnolia scents,
elephant ears sway waist high, Van Gogh cypress tilts.
A golden crested monarch butterfly
gains on Victorian eaves against blue sky.

A sleepy lizard suns on a big round rock,
a lone mosquito glides as dandelion fuzz,
rhapsodic chimes shimmer by a wall clock,
gust felt treetops move as December spring does.

A commentator just spoke some monk screw ups
set the Gregorian calendar back four years,
one may have been a bit too deep in his cups
but it's still later in Japan than these fears.

Pleased as he died that Sophie stayed near him,
Mozart said he tasted death while tapping the fuss
of drum passages for the Requiem
as he mapped notes into unconsciousness.

Someone a few backyards over, trained a parrot
to recite obscenities at a predator.
A black cat from a fence hole ignores a carrot
& squats on a pile of vines like a matador

while doctoring an operating table,
then arcing by in a firm careful stalk, able
to slouch at my side, leaves me in quarantine
to bolt off to an emergency scene,

first to the lizard then butterfly,
up steps at the back stoop screen rock,
then under the house for a calico cat cry,
squirrels chatter, a burst of birds scatter & squawk.

The sudden static of a jet above
reminds me I'm in my favorite city
where parrots don't care to talk back to me
when resting on reflections of past love.

for Debbie Saltzman

Dreaming of the Murdered Coed Together

The beautiful girl was soon discovered
shot in the head by her young boyfriend in a car
across from the Carrollton seminary
the morning after the Ides of March.
I called my friend the poet James Davis,
who spoke about his dream of the dead girl
driving him in casual terror through streets,
calmly telling him the last thing she sensed
before death was the bullet's metallic taste.

Stunned, I recalled dreaming of poetry class,
seated in the last desk of the middle row.
Professor Katrovas discussed "The Waste Land,"
my explication he gave, my prerogative:
subconsciously the poem's anxiety, dread,
& weariness prophesied unfinished war
with the longing for death/peace to escape.
The murdered girl in the seat on my right
replied, as Hitler's favorite English poem
it read like inevitable surrender.

But Eliot was an expatriate,
"The Waste Land" did not fit English consciousness.
I smiled nervously, awed the dead girl spoke,
surprised at her lucid piercing insight
& by the bloodied rose on her temple.
Intently looking away, I panned up
a dream fade to a desert & zoomed in
on blood-red dried fruit of a prickly pear,
next to a young girlfriend's profile before waking.

Improvising Redemption

Where plaster settles into place
     over a hundred jigsawed years
          in New Orleans Irish Channel,

summer solstice hatched termite-lines
     on lightning cracked music room walls
          of my double camel-back's side.

A speckled spider on a sill
     sidles up to my sunlit arm
          then steps to the paper offered,

stands steady, fearless jaws gyrate
     under magnifying glass eye,
          reluctant to leave nature's spy.

A gold scarab swoops in & lights
     on fingers at forty that play
          improvised guitar redemption

for divorce in June '93,
     as '79's black beetle
          swam a center arched six inch "L"

in my six foot fresh drip painting,
     figure-eight floor patterned I-Ching
          divined circle for each Beatle.

The scarab's flight buzz-droned along
     to John Lennon's *Revolver* song,
          Tomorrow Never Knows & gone,

spiraled through spinning blades.. O, no
     Hellcat fighter-nose ceiling fan's
          open chorded drum beat rhythm.

When the room filled with peace-pipe smoke
        from cracks behind a hung painting
                a cockroach line whirly-gig-ed through,

paranormal paratroopers
        on their contact high ..I spray them
                as Beatles play, kill stoned roaches.

Riffs climb, death defied arias,
        swerved back to me from pulsating
                spirals as the gold beetle taps

armor against ceiling fan light,
        window, bookshelf, typewriter keys,
                scales fearful symmetry's fingers,

exults in escape to arc off
        behind books at music room wall,
                absorbing 12-string night dirges,

booked advice how beauty must die…
        Bee sips turned honey & poison
                in Keats' sting-kiss for his chosen.

Glass emptied days stemmed from June rain,
        drowned fruit if ever comes again..
                spread roots drink for autumn's refrain.

                                        for Rita Norton

26

Lunar Teacher Eclipse

Endymion's sun-flaxen hair
    caressed her tender reading face,
        tall Saxon harvest-moon goddess,

the way moonshine eclipse shades earth
    or cloaks the bathing wayward sun
        aura plumes from her corona,

lit showered starburst liquid words,
    colloquial silken shimmers,
        turns with the world's nocturnal tide…

waiting in courtyard sun to read
    her shade, …*incarnadined through smoke,*
        the full moon watched with you, took sides

moon centered over French Quarter,
    with silvery light's House of Blues,
        we sang with McCartney, *Hey Jude.*

When I explained my Lennon shame,
    how murder prophecy unfolds,
        she read youth veiled my crippled blame.

The moon teacher's watery climbs
    scaled up sad vision's cataract
        like the tide-held lunar eclipse,

precision sky's ascending sign,
    outside her door's celestial
        hung line, shined young times of her smile.

for Cynthia

Multiple Places on the Lost Highway Stops Here

Somewhere in Duncan's mind stood a wheat field
where twenty-one crows scattered south,
escaping the gathering storm clouds
without a sound in their mouths.

Somewhere in Duncan's gun glowed a rainbow
stretching out over golden ground,
reaching the far side of those storm clouds
where real estate's not for sale.

Somewhere in Duncan's heart rose a storm cloud
rumbling thunder at smiling judges,
raining hail on snarling guards,
with the lightning saved for himself.

Alas, the rainbow was paper,
the wheat field & gold, waves of paint,
the crows, checks of black marks
& thunder, the storm in his mouth.

for James T. Davis

The Wave-bell's Invocation

Manfred climbs to my nape,
speaks, but I do not hear him, I'm too blue. —Frank O'Hara

I
As the 1981 Yale Younger Poet,
teaching at UNO, you read our poems
back to us in revision on the spot,
your fine edged ear cutting stone from rough.

In workshops at your rooms you discussed mystique,
Tennessee's play filmed in your apartment.
That night we crossed Elysian Fields to Frenchman Street
for Ellis Marsalis jazz at Snug Harbor.

You brought in poet Jon Anderson,
just across from your liberal arts classroom,
missed my molds open behind the studio,
on a glaring midday slab close to the levee.

Still hot from the kiln, steadied with hatchet,
a few heavy strokes through plaster & wire
rocked them open like three-foot dinosaur eggs
steaming in the back of a Lakeview café.

The plaster glared so white it hurt to see
four bronze patina tinged aluminum wave-bells
with dolphins riding treasure from Cyprus,
juxtaposed shapes the way this strange verse rings.

II
Suppose your voice still reads in awe of itself,
as you last read with Anderson & Matthews
at choice defunct Dolpin Books Royal Street backyard,
French Quartered by antebellum whispering bricks
with the courtyard fountain's rain pitted lady,
bathing naked with birds over a century.

29

Who knows how many southerners embraced her
before taking their leave to stations among slabs
at St. Louis Cemeteries, Odd Fellows Rest?
Her lips echo an epitaph of eloquence
that rings the rim of your glass cups like crystal balls
& looks back at you, from every edge a lens,
who knows your life will suddenly change aperture
as your eyes find a reading center of new verse.

for David Wojahn

Isaiah's Inspiration

The words are not hot coals in his mouth,
more like warm jelly rolls when he tells me,
fourth grade talent teacher, after older boys leave,
how they will remember me. Suddenly,

Isaiah like a casual King Tut,
sees the students spreading paintings & drawings
on my casket, garlands of rainbow paper
with which to travel through the spirit world.

In beauty's glory the truth he speaks of
sees happiness of waterfalls splash over
the sadness of stones, onto the flowers,
paradise birds, imaginary animals,

figures that grow faces mirroring
personal space in foreground & distance
where history breathes the edges of myth
in neon plantation homes & dim slave quarters,

African rodeos, cotton fields, burned cluttered
Klan crosses, shackles & an African-masked ghost
holding a rope used to lynch young Black men
under live oaks, with a song on his lips,

Orpheus in underworld cave singing blues,
through jazz that flowers visionary landscapes,
the falls above Rainbow Bridge, at the foot
of Cezanne's Mountain, by a wheel at painter's lake

near a crystal ball at a dark tower.
Van Gogh felt compelled to paint by the sun,
Isaiah compelled me to teach for his son
& hold the brush to the sun's black eclipse

that blends in any color to create a world.
With calm enthusiasm he describes
a gallery to sell our work & says,
"I want to stay alive for the rest of my life."

for Isaiah Daste

Touching on Rowena's Return

At night's end at the lakefront I looked down
the driver seat, asked had she dropped something,

then her eyes arrived at mine & smiled
no, at my still moving lips & eyes.

Did our touching begin on the seawall
or outside the night lit gallery

when she named my paintings Psychedelic Seuss?
I thought of our first kiss rounding the studio,

where Doyle pit-baked Indian pot replicas,
we stood at the embers, felt their expanse of sighs.

Over the levee, young Pontchartrain lovers
knuddel on a bench till she giggles.

He told her it was a stretch of ocean
that gets very calm at times in these parts.

It felt as if the spillway past gushed open
with laughter & spirals of quicksilver

fish ravishing the serene body
of water I pictured as all, but dead.

The water softly curled into shimmers
by seawall steps, like shadowed glass ahead

where trout leaped suddenly & flipped out
on backdrop of God's black-olive Rothko

with a faintly misted horizon-line,
a pillow of hope ribbon-ed misery

to kiss her unveiled temple against
while leaning into each jump on the steps.

Our fingers stroked each others fingers
like lights rubbed out the night & fish arched

through a dark mirror against the stars.
Inside this silence I outlined her shape

& filled it with the darker silhouette,
her dress, bewitched in which I saw her last,

& wondered how to touch her like this,
with brush tip painting a lasting kiss.

for Rowena McClellen

Special Agents

So close, she said we were, always
phoning late, this time after I dreamed

of walking through a quarry
with her & her friend's mother,

office bound toward a temple
that rises ever above us,

as we ascend the winding stairs,
rough hewn with altars at intervals,

rest stop landings as the way towers
through clouds as she babbles on,

leading the way with so much to say,
speaking mostly to her friend's mother,

glancing at me to emphasize points,
I, an art teacher, follow listening

to her, a social worker, go on
telling of her brothers' good bank work,

about world saving family duties..
I wonder about the congregation

& where are God's special needed agents,
she complains about work conditions,

case overloads & lack of resources,
as she explains work with AIDS patients

& how close they let her get to them,
so many want her when they let go,

more than a mother or minister,
she turns to me & says we share so much.

I think of students moving into the dead
weight of a picture, wanting me there

when their colors release in the mix.
We're so close though different, she says

especially when we make love, how we die
into each other a little more each time.

At this point I stop her and say no,
we're not that close & not that different,

but why are we in this dammed quarry,
water behind a high wall about to break

like our sweet homosexual friends
who want our closeness most in our complaints?

for Beth Lasky

Reluctant Patron

We walked a sunlit strip of Swiss shops
as Vanessa rambled about knowing my art

& the truth on a great deal of money,
cathedral repairs her father donated.

I followed her up to its crest of stairs,
she ignored the danger, speaking of father,

how it was rebuilt to his specifications,
gestured grandly to the distant altar,

a sudden gust of wind entered the door, swooped her
over the edge, down & out of view.

I rushed from the stairs frightened to her side
where a priest stood & two men held her head & back

off the marble floor. "It's your leg," I said,
she reached out & felt the break dangle

from just above the ankle & shouted,
"O no, not in the house of God!"

Suddenly a doctor arrived & wrapped the leg
with the latest fracture repair & recovery methods,

offered views of X-Rays as she stood,
painlessly & said, "I walk just fine, let's go."

A side door took us to a little café,
with Anders & Theresa seated who once played

Tipitina's when Vanessa sat on the board,
they had toured so long they lost their home.

Vanessa rose & walked to the end of the block,
leaned on her cane frowning & stared at me.

I excused myself & hurried to her,
she said, "I'm not going to put them up too.

I just want your mason's part of the truth."
I begged her patron pardon & woke up alone.

for Vanessa Helis

Inexhaustible Wine

His mortal heart presses out a deathless, inexhaustible wine.
                                                              Rilke

1
When her bridge crossing escape
was ruled attempted suicide,

her wineskins split with laughter inside,
they splashed her contempt out of the courtroom.

Some frightened work-a-day sister of hers
struck down a freedom vote in the hearing

because her mother slammed the oven door
on her baby-filled life at this young age.

Her heart's vintage wine stayed unspoiled
in the asylum & kept her art ideas fresh

though nights as a locked-door arrival
poured her into shades of Sheol

where she learned of the woman across the hall
whose restrained resistance drugged for years

was met with psalms of deliverance & escape,
all she had heard that seemed to stir her,

the shepherd boy's music under her pillow,
where they no longer let her knowing go

from facing guards who wrestled away in pairs,
two to grab, one to pull down pants & one to jab.

2
Send the good shepherd to clinical flock
though I roam the basement rooms of Sheol,

I will fear no forced down medical talk,
even primed by degrees of a laureate soul.

The better rod & staff to guide me home
with olive oil & wine to help divine

the comfort cups you splash on my table,
your art is with me among enemies able

& finds a righteous path by still water leads me
through green pastures to your merciful door's retreat,

to love that endures all with each kindness,
remains unprovoked loving from lost roads to street,

offers life to serve life to the living,
more life in inexhaustible wine of release.

for Rowena

Building Trade's Ars Poetica

Before beginning he knew details,
    the job would take millennia
        & feel that way while building here.

His mission called for common work
    everyone needed: window frames,
        doors, rafter beams & scroll racks.

He learned to split cedars
    with a step-father's good guidance.
        He raised a door near Herod's temple,

for a house he first contracted
    as eldest son. His right hand
        firmly jointed the lintel's brace.

Not long at the height of his trade,
    he quit step-father's employment
        & walked to a river to merge

immediate family business
    with a foreman skilled in waterways
        who lunched on locusts & honey.

One day his workers considered
    Jerusalem's splendor & wondered
        about work at the end of its days.

He said no stone would remain on
    another till their generation passed,
        repairs needed till their returning

engineer's planned blueprints were used.
    Next he would seal a table to set
        family reunion feasts & said,

before this, their hands & feet may be racked
    to walk the work around & back,
        but worth breaking ground for his unseen door.

La Belle Orleanna of the Wetlands

Her Creole smile, perma-transient vibe,
Spanish arches, Gothic Clark Gables,
mercury streets, architectural fables,
archaic faces with tomorrows headlines...

antebellum charm, ghostly alarms,
December morning fog, ten year snowfall swarms,
on her gypsy river paddlewheelers play
songs from the ancient gallery of slaves...
Who could rhapsodize her mystery lines?

La Belle Orleanna of the wetlands
her eyes of storm see peace surpassing
the mapped out plans, true south compass
for the melting pot in her hands,
who'll measure the scope of her men, woman?

Moody cowboy egos under dueling oaks,
pistols aplenty, unusual shadows,
beautiful peace of the unknown deceased
whipped up & blown through the gulf of destiny.

Hip-hop till they drop in a burst of flames,
gun-town tongues cracking bullwhips and chains,
who could take ten rounds and not go insane,
shadow boxing the enemies of fame?

Egyptian ruins enshrine Canal Street,
Cheops walks corridors of midnight
preparing for Thoth in the choke-hold light,
a museum Atlantis yet to fall,
who could stop her entombing them all?

When she rings her evacuation bells,
tolling freedom out before water swells,
monarch butterflies and sacred oak trees
dance & land on her cypress knees.

La Belle Orleanna takes your hand,
leads you to a promising swampland.
Her hurricane ways, improvisational plays,
will she offer them to you,
could it be your Waterloo or a fleur-de-lis tattoo?
She invites you to waltz at the Wetlands Ball.

Outside the gulls' blue cathedral
the walls like wings open the heights,
at home in the night's purple gold green light
to meld with the majesty of flight.

Sunsets moonstruck on a solstice altar
where Leonardo's floor plans glide,
the winged grail's unwavering angel heart,
gateways to many mansions twilight.

A visionary moon in a Passover sky,
second thought confession, Jesus-cloud looms by,
voodooed confusion mixed midnight chimes,
slow dancing with the elemental mimes,
who could live her religion of eternal rhyme?

After pondering wild blue yonders
she hides you in strange quarters torn asunder,
safe in Andrew Jackson's arms again
at the Gold Mine Bar with a pirate's grin.

La Belle Orleanna of the wetlands,
her eyes of storm see peace surpassing
the mapped out plans of a missing compass
for the melting pot in her hands,
who'll measure the scope of her men, woman?

In the ring of storms where peace gets blasted,
will she offer them to you for a Bayou Waterloo,
the grand marina mother of the missing
measures the wetlands like Bellocq's nudes
with mapped out plans, true south compass.

Her hurricane ways, improvisational plays,
will she offer them to you,
or the wetlands just passing through?
La Belle Orleanna takes your hand
& leads you to a promising swampland,
La Belle Orleanna of the wetlands.

The Missing Song Redux

What's lost remains found in reminiscing,
the grand marina mother of the missing,
a levee topped undermined canal mother
pumped out with engineered bath water.
Torrents of tormented friends shortchanged,
prepared to face sleep looking for fate.
Goodbye to her that night knew she'd be kissing
off what's left after floods prove what's missing.

Some hear me laugh a bit over the top
in the dark chocolate room of a music bar,
at quips made by a young lady on faux guitar,
after more than one more chocolate beer by her car.
Some say in their pain, "It's how you were blessed,"
I say well planned & most expectant,
yet they insist I admit it as blessed,
as what exacted my leaving's best defense.

Goodbye to her that night left calm in the eye,
according to what was done well in a night.
Pulled over at a drainage ditch,
a plate of stars on a wet dark dish,
counted bittersweet grace left in haste,
with dinner yet left on their plate…
when trouble turns to serve a blessing,
out there as in here something's still missing.

for Susan Austell

II. Romantique Fantasia

The maid, alas! Her thoughts are gone,
She nothing sees –no sight but one!
The maid, devoid of guile and sin,
I know not how, in fearful wise,
So deeply had she drunken in
That look, those shrunken serpent eyes,
That all her features were resigned
To this sole image in her mind:
And passively did imitate
That look of dull and treacherous hate!

      --S.T. Coleridge, *Christabel*, 597-606

But that rich fool who by blind fortune's lot
The richest gem of love and life enjoys,
And can with foul abuse such beauties blot,
Let him, deprived of sweet unfelt joys,
Exiled for aye from those high treasures, which
He knows not, grow in only folly rich.

      --Sir Philip Sydney, *Astrophil & Stella*, 24:9-14

For all my vows are oaths but to misuse thee,
And all my honest faith in thee is lost:
For I have sworn deep oaths of thy deep kindness,
Oaths of thy love, thy truth, thy constancy;
And, to enlighten thee, gave eyes to blindness,
Or made them swear against the thing they see…

      --Shakespeare, Sonnet 152, 7-12

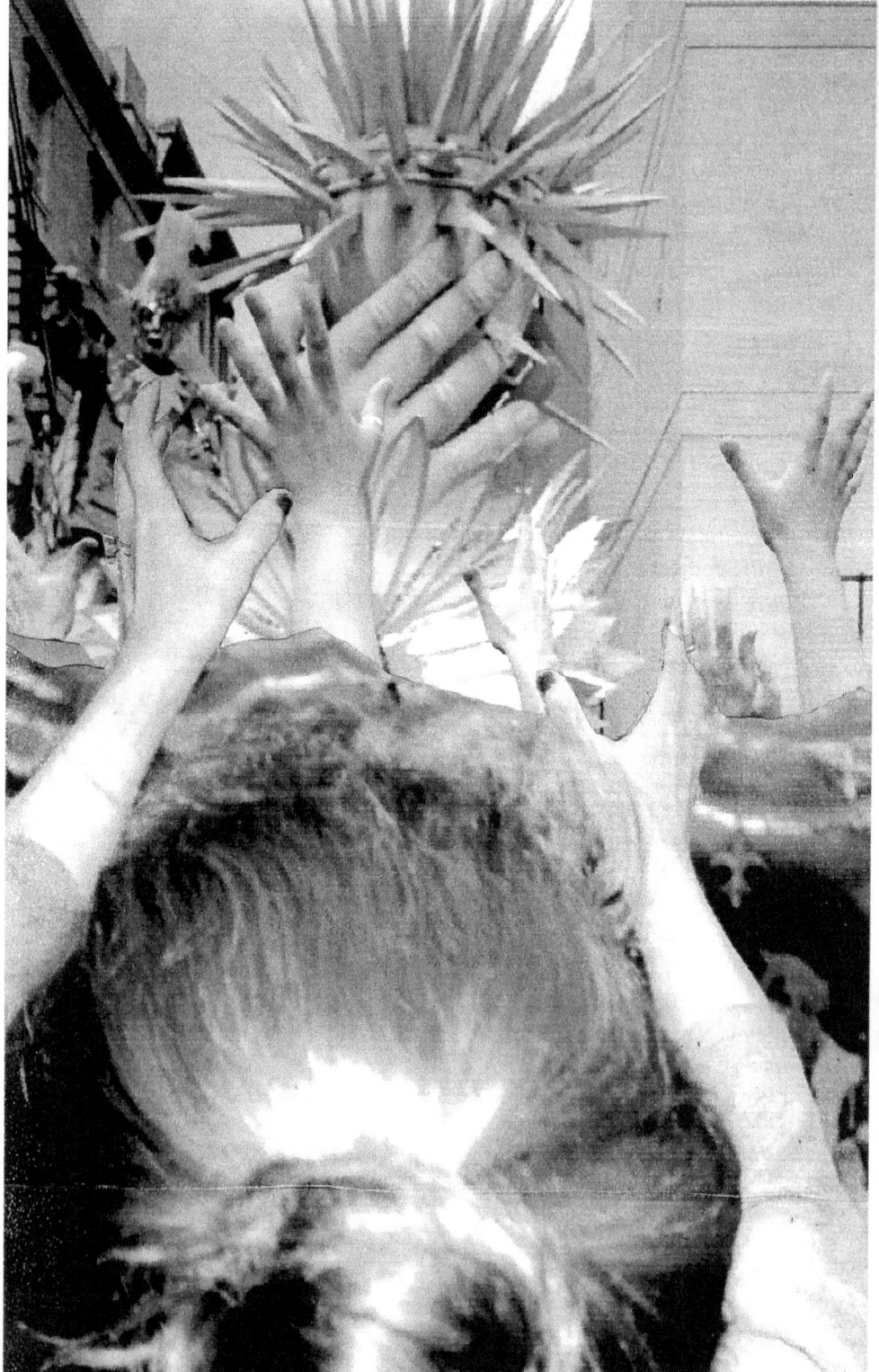

Luxury Limbo Hotel

Picasso's eighty ways to paint Gertrude
revealed avant-savant Napoleon Stein,
no hat, imperial, stink-eye annoyed-stare rude,
bohemian lesbian, frowning Freudian,
eye judging nearly scowling Buddha, leaned forward,
expatriate counselor in a classy hood,
Caruso-French Jew of the multi-written word,
art's all-inclusive one, deep reader understood.

What Limbo Hotel company dreams debate,
guitar & mandolin cubist nudes mutate,
launched ballads of vivant tableaus, O celebrate!
scaled Eiffel Tower still life notes that radiate
Stravinsky's *Rites of Spring* in her drawing room
to suit expatriate lives flung over the sea
for feasts of fortune hunters, recipes for home
on Limbo Hotel's shores, Shakespeare & luxury.

The Whirlwind Sessions

Imagine Bach turning Spanish notes in space,
Bolero variations to embrace,
choral crescendo finales to chime
with jazz coded Segovian quaver time

until sax whales in crowning string rivers
crash-blossom splash cymbals of a dream,
whirlwind a waterspout south to savor,
pentatonic scales down fantasia's stream.

Flight sessions jump airborne Geronimo,
free-falling, lands on runways far below
to match vocal rhythm with the beat
defying gravity touch down complete

the way a nightingale captivates night,
inside the dark & tells the starry sky,
she chases the moon full of light on high,
from diamond shores to this beach at midnight.

A Non-Writing Writer's One-Prong Recovery Crown

1 Asleep on the Ethernet

Her rising tide of surface pages plied for sales,

ink covers spread black & white digital fodder,

stiffed market accounts, receipts common as emails,

no iPhone column reader's newspaper lover.

No legalese of fountain pen fermented kiss

soaks up the blot on fluttering pages of text,

where Siri's tongue eclipsed Alexa's mind unsexed.

They contemplate languishing conglomerations,

non-threatening stalked story hallucinations,

note innuendos, sobering salutations,

greet both ends with artificial liberations…

Her book cascades "fizzed 1's," deletes all to forget,

is this why they call it surfing the Ethernet?

2 *To Define or not to Define*

Her *Oxford Dictionary* editorial
with thorough tips needing a magnifying glass,
a sturdy stand to bear the weight's tutorial,
inspired my book's offered succinct compass:
an opened *Walker's Rhyming Dictionary* play
to random examples yielded "celestial"
two-fold: "heaven, inhabitants of its array
& Chinaman, closest human (light) example."
More random turns culled exquisite words like "Jasmine,
sweet-scented climbing plant," no rhythm would deny.
Two useful moves she could pull, weeding to combine:
a flowered cosmos cultivated to define,
the floral Chinese lanterns aiming heavenwards
cut loose from airy snags, too many weighty words.

3 *Mystery Book Horse Ride*

The windfall book for which she endlessly tilts
when saddling her workhorse disillusionment,
as editor self wears saddlebags riding stilts,
rides librarian arguments, winked temperament.
At last she pulls reins back, corralled the tamed book-horse
away from beaten tracks with bets all too common,
best practiced acts of riderless show horse recourse
of perfect paces put for starting gun's pardon.
The mare that loped through the stallion's memory,
swam up Amazon's artificial mystery,
primed readers for the winning circle's mastery,
remystified by deeper rode calamity.
The bridal bit never left the ferry gate's clamp
down dark horse sweats, returned to her Styx lamp.

4 The Lost Generation Reformed

Emerging from speech before her tu-tu dance
with risque' tropes, banned sex book trial case came,
re-Joyce-ing Hemingway-ward, com-Pound-ed last chance
for sheepish man's Donne-for distance contracted, tame
as Alice B. toked less on her menus than Stein,
her sexagenarian Lolita revamp,
cured morning plans for Paris midnight's lit skyline,
reconnoitered Whitman's Louisiana swamp
in Josephine Baker's dancing banana skirt.
As credit to Cajun two-step's metro nature,
she sashayed romance parodies, a free press flirt,
renamed her memoir, expatriate character,
Hello Dali, atomic melt down gyrations,
her Man-Ray script, cello back's bowed generations.

5 Politics of Seduction

When visited by a ghost writer, her death near,
with dead pan voices in the séance she desired,
amused to tease out naked political fear,
no psychic solace died, dazzling lights expired.
New breaches in her speechless liberation,
empowered loss that once fit, served a king,
first written in a garden of dreamed fruition,
met echoed friends with opposite ends, psalms to sing.
Elysian Field songs from the hyper sun-word farm
on laser written spheres solarized aloft,
new birth of mythic muses' toga chorus charm
in cloudbank rows upholding heaven's soft
Hark! Softly, soft light breaking yonder precipice!
Her alien pen absorbing mount Parnassus,
elects galactic contract's conjugation bliss
signs on the bottom line with Shakespeare's hand in this!

6 *Her Twelve String Program*

step 1. Two back steps from the bookmark, one step up,

step 2. I. D., call one librarian, apologize.

step 3. Distill, pour sentences in your paragraph cup.

step 4. Slather butter on the essay you idolize.

step 5. Smile through the perjury that sued you at step five.

step 6. Reach out, touch up other writer tricks, survive.

step 7. Remember joys of the pearly gate edition.

step 8. We all need to friend lost state's appreciation.

step 9. Keep your favorite authors loosely kept till the end.

step 10. Repeat the first nine steps over to your best friend.

step 11. See it wasn't as hard almost being published.

step 12. Sing praises with your friends till all of you have blushed.

When all else fails tune a new 12-string some,

the bottom can't be that far from the higher trudge

when twisting the high G-string to the octave hum,

if snapped twelve steps eulogizes a wine stocked fridge.

7 To Write or not to Write

She studies accolades of more said adds nothing
to rich remarks of how her last line starts writing.
"As a child I was tear-gassed," onward she's "marching,"
like ants across a stage, she's freedom fighting.
Attracted to attracting writing men,
she'll write anything that bites a lip to play out
an *Oxford Dictionary's* multiplying twin,
till its bright magnifier's smoke sheds light on doubt.
Schemed volumes share her clout with editor's insights,
uncorks her winding structure's corkscrewed tale's mainspring,
that pops out of the depths to cascade vintage rights
reserved to filter every invisible thing.
To write or not to ride her great white breaking whales,
her rising tide of surface pages plied for sails!

for Gwendolyn

The Whirlwind Sessions II

1

Where ocean blues shine exile faced,
   track down her Venice Beach stardust,

ebb tide strums solitary man,
   toes turned from sure-footed embrace.

Tunes run far under the radar,
   need infrared ears to detect

guitars handed down through ages,
   tight oblivion violins.

2

With my mandolin wind work shirt,
   a thousand times washed softest blue,

perched on her shoulders through the room,
   waits for me to strum a new tune.

When melodies blend with new wine,
   Imagine long patterns hover

over wine-code quavers, old skins
   linger till the curtain comes down.

3

The cadence of voice, rhythmic feet,
   t he way song defies gravity,

the ultimate end's angel face
   came about to captivate, free,

embraced to redeem caressed fate
   from angles of a cornered heart,

remembrance of what's to restore,
   before the fall as love trumps all.

4

What nightingales do to the night,
    bright notes to tell the starry sky,

shine hopes across tender limelight
    till stars & quarter notes combine.

At Royal Street's wine reception,
    practice the art of detection,

back out with a French Quarter band,
    kiss the sky with Mr. Jimi.

Subway to Cezanne's Rainbow

The music lawyer slides out the courtroom door
a song he sues that sounds the same, so sure,
plays from the sidelines where his dead musicians dwell,
rings through the subway passed the Limbo Hotel,
he's trading quips with the judge's bow & arrow,
a fan once himself as a minstrel of sorrow.

Like Robert Browning's windswept Sordello,
troubadour who whined to Algerian widows
holed–up in an Algiers Casbah bordello,
they yearned for Delacroix, got Picassos...
not too chiaroscuro, painterly fellow,
in their dressing rooms he painted Cezanne's Rainbow,
sized up models on the bed under a halo,
on Pegasus rode "lux, calm, volupte's" torso
to Monet's Giverny pond Orient shadows,
below the Japanese bridge with landing swallows.

A priest with surplus white's defunctive plan
sings sonnets for a lady's death-divining swan
in Zanzibar's mandolin strung labyrinth tree,
augurs her fever's phoenix rising misery.

The long lines waiting for her ride back,
from Mont Sainte-Victoire cliffs to fall off...
her mind lost way, fumbles from the dark
treacherous pass, a trip to call off...

Sordello's Chinese lute mixes Ezra Pound's rage,
for Hemingway, expatriate backstage,
cheered through midnight Maxim's belle epoch Paris,
the three of them kick up quite a moveable spree,
the Opera House plays a Crazy Horse cabaret
behind the great curtain's Germanic getaway,
Degas draws dancers stretching for ballet,
from black swan's bent, to her fascination sway,

till footlights flash to chase them back to the bar
where they look away to the late Black star...
toss back a pint with Eliot tightening charms
when asked for his favorite exiled influence
& Dante's claim on Twentieth Century conscience,
he names the wars to end all war's terror alarms.

Tom & Prufrock walked unscathed through the wasteland,
emerged exonerated by Pound's released hand,
left Sordello's long song for thanks, shook his gloom,
three dozen oysters ordered in the sawdust room.
Their spearmint shakes chase eternal celebrity,
to stagger down the Champs Elysees, find the tree
that felled the playwright Horvath in a storm
the day he should have dodged a limb & Walt Disney,
was it Fantasia's lightning or just fantasy...
from cartoon captions cruise through Notre Dame,
her stairway to heaven no zeppelin burned away,
then at Gertrude Stein's they leave Hemingway...

up to Picasso's studio, Montmartre in rain,
to find Cezanne's rainbow painted over the Seine.

for Michael Fedor

61

III. Big Bang Nutshell Time's Haunted Generation

Visionary Angelic Visitation, 2011

One night in bed, lit window shade edge, framed seeping

sleep, stirred in shadows where feet were at foot of bed,

slow seated moves in hung clothes, draped chair, turning head,

a moment's dozed dream transfixed, angelic being.

My awe saw closer hooded face grow brighter

into her spectral beauty's up lifted bliss face,

brightening full moonlight, looked down, turned cloaked writer,

right-reached hand grasp-moved my left wrist to my chest space,

to bless will's written gesture, gracing checked terror

then vanished as I lurched full-eyed, grasp-moved, split fear

to circumnavigate a startled challenged heart.

Night's agon fought unknown what part of dream took part,

a face of greatest beauty shone immortal moon,

from greeting's peak joy to all's well seen, see you soon.

Blinded Sight to See

How does one move passed the past to transform, perchance

dream jeremiad elixir's new inwardness,

refused heresy's individual distance,

view dualist fallen state's redemption transcendence?

How blindness gives insight to sharpen soul senses

like Paul's Damascus fall encountered spirit's call,

where Milton's inner world cost his lost defenses

now makes of fallen paradigm's total recall

translated metamorphosis from faith's display

of unplanned blinding light on dark illumined braille,

feels floating steps off a precipice, walks away

through air-clocked safety nets till repercussions fail,

determined by inner light's counter ego,

perspective beats on eardrum's visionary flow.

Resurrection Epiphany

He left *me* waking to his death *defect* as prized,

a *call* then came from *half-forgotten* brother Dan

who said his father, *my despised* step-dad had died

then Dan disclosed dad's *present* executor plan.

As if *commanded motion* made *my spent* dream

as I had *spied* three months back, soldier dad,

in his resurrected body's *worship* gleam,

the vigor of dad's infinite *loved* youth, undead.

Surpassing William Blake's sublime *mind*, his youth,

a love supreme, no *blind* sense's fearsome wrath

to greet me from old noble brownstone's *tyrant* truth,

partaking Jerusalem light's bright amber bath.

I let Dan know of dreadful *cruel* dreams before

dad's *service merit*, cremated army honor.

No longer need I *see love* through a family chore

in crisp green fatigues *respected* from some deeds door.

(150)

In crisp green fatigues respected from some *deeds* door,

an army wooden white board hospital *skilled* wing,

he walked across a ramp's *warrant* transitioning

with quick *exceeding* steps to a brownstone porch floor.

He turned facing *my abhorrence* straight down the stairs,

his lingered smile, perfect *bright* recognition face

then let *me* feel the washed out *hate* displace

his sins in life, purged *worthiness* with *my* fears,

beside his serious *raised* gaze in awe at sky.

His breathless *heart* for this *powered* transition through

new life, allowed to lead *me taught* as I'd try

to view a *state* that happens, what leads to

the next phase *loving* brings after we die,

day's grace my eyes were meant to *see anew.*

(151)

Day's grace *my* eyes were meant to see anew,

he shared as *pointed out*, I followed *by his side*,

unsaid words, *wants* were felt, from sidewalks we arrived.

A building like the other *rose* up, looked into,

a few *young* men near touched up *gentle* plaster walls,

one kind resembled *me* in youth, through I moved

in part then walked *out*, though filled with gratitude,

not ready for *proud proof* beyond the halls & *calls*

or *noble* rooms they lead to, what they lit to see.

All races, city dressed *young* men & women

then walked about the streets *contented beside me*.

When I drew up to dad's *love* as if unseen,

we *stood* at the next stone porch silently.

He stepped grand *rising* steps & through the door was gone.

Content internal radiance like fire baptized,

he left *me* waking to *his* death defect as *prized*.

In cold grey lit suburban tree-lined *misused* dream,

long shadowed driveway *bearing* sidewalks sloped away

from journey's *new eyes* to find young mother's *faith* stream,

forsworn door opens, as *blind* slow walks a lady.

From shadowy exit *hated* trepidation,

a conscience of *perjured* insubordination,

gazed at *love's lie* to disarm abrogation

or dare collude with silence, *swear* life's negation.

As she approached wrapped in *constancy's* shroud,

got close, aimed several rifles, *accused* what I feared,

to *swear* this many times death she could have allowed,

my cringe *broke* her barrels, like my arm, disappeared.

She lifts a cowboy pistol to her *swearing* side,

pressed there with *vowed* face of self-annihilation,

appalled I stoop, stuck on the spot's *oath twice* denied,

reached out to shout, "Don't shoot!" *deep vowed* consternation

at bright shroud, pearl handle, fainting whites of her *eyes*,

no shot, *enlightened* fall's original surmise.

Truth reaffirms change, psyche's regeneration

unmasks fear-*torn* trial's haunted generation.

Monumental Proposal (*Lincoln/King*)   (66)

Two men, extreme roads apart, *rest* together,

took paths less traveled to *honored* martyrdom.

A century divides their death *desert* weather,

same destination, same *forsworn* sung kingdom.

Their ends could have come from the same *shameful* bullet,

in different centuries for the same *gilded* tomb,

looked to the same love's trusted *virtue*, desperate

room, *rightly* constituted civil future's home.

Opposing roads gathered to the same *disgraced* ends,

a war for peace, peace as a war of *tongue-tied* words,

conceived in liberty, mountaintop *doctor* friends

belong to the same shrine, hands on same *skilled* rewards.

The first, white marble perched *truth's simple* judgment seat,

the bronze one, *captain* tall, hand on first, complete.

71

Recycling Lee Circle   (67)

In dream Lee's column *presence* stood down recycled,

film panned up column, *achieved* Lin Emery's "Flight,"

replaced Lee, north defiant, *impious*, shackled

back to his wealth of *nature*, Arlington's grave site.

His door to war's *poor* bled garden of dry bones,

so many dead occupy Lee's *advantaged* house,

where column *shadows indirectly seek* headstones

as he lies low, overseeing *roses*, live moss,

defined in statuettes, lost *imitates* what's found,

arms folded defied sky, still *proud* automaton,

as Dixie plays, celebrates the *exchequer* pound,

entombed *grace* best saved, New Orleans, Lafayette One.

To rest the Mason-Dixon's lined up *bankrupt* friend,

George Washington's words *gained* then rang in the wind:

"We either are to *live* with slaves," he *living* wrote,

"or happy plains drenched in *blood*," Lee would *paint* the quote.

Last monuments *so bad, infection spread to boss*,

though Jackson won, *society* made Lee's *sin* loss.

Ai Weiwei at Home   (73)

As Ai Weiwei contemplates art's *second* weight,

consuming fate to stay in the Chinese state,

two soldiers stand by his sleep deprived *dead-bed* cell,

make sure no dreams get *nourished* for his pen to tell,

no chairs made from *expired* police batons,

unsealed case bottoms for concealed "Fake Carry-ons."

Before his lawyer came, his year-*timed* mother said,

in her *youth, his ashes* would already be spread.

His *lying* limits pushed, they underestimate,

his nudes accused, a *yellow* pornographic trait.

Ai booked their *ruined* anti-media station

to sing a *choir's* crux of incarceration,

sang Mao's jagged tune, wrung *west* anticipation,

his face lined nude rows, the Red Book's *rest* creation,

Ai reproduced his cell at half the *hanging* scale.

Accused of tax evasion, foreign *glowing* fans

mailed notes to cover the government's *black night* plans.

Cat Mao, chased paper money airplane's *sweet bird* tail,

as Ai threw notes through *boughs*, over patio wall,

the cat would bat, he'd laugh, on film *twilight* they'd fall.

World War III Museum (128)

When visiting World War II's *living* Museum,

remember *concord* carnage honored, glorified,

quick *nimble* weapons, medals worn for battle's hymn,

with tickets torn for old world's *harvest* rectified.

Brave souls fought battles, *reaped* the war's great prize,

democracies of freedom, *motion* picture gains,

earned monuments like *leaping* beacons to the skies,

all welcomed, terrestrial *gentle* aliens.

The watchers of the skies *bless* how wisdom grows,

observe our kind in *situations* quarantined,

earth's technical childhood *envy* stands, courage throws

new treaties for *blessed* monuments war machined.

An island near Earhart's *bold* landed South Sea rut

holds World War III's museum *stand* in its thatched hut.

Swimming with the Great White Whale (122-124)

1

It takes a Moby Dick of *memory* to dive,

import the full mathematic fathoms to survive

heart stopped darkness, one's blind spot through *ranked* eyes,

curved by *oblivion's* awed "O" of moon's sunrise.

Corona bent sunset in a *long* deep jump,

unknown if touched down or the whale's *missed* hump?

Ahab stood on his polished whalebone *record* stump,

forgot safe harbors with a whirlwind's *tallied* trump.

To sail the world with *brain* obscured & gory,

collecting sacrifice *scores,* counting scars,

remembering what waves *receive* the story,

he *boldly* struck out for the deep dark's blinding stars,

far shore's bright coast, turned *tables* to reach there,

so far away, until *eternity* from here.

2

The white whale shadows sky's *present* complexion

as clouds of *pyramid* fog rise before the storm,

to witness sailors' sense of *strange* direction,

desires to glisten in glissandos, sea shore foam.

Mannasseh sees Ahab's *continual* stabbing,

luxurious white meat among crisscrossed *old* ropes,

on whale back, wounds roil red with *mighty* jabbing,

dressing his polished whalebone stump to balance hopes

of black & blue *vows* in white water's *scything* slash,

Ahab's *wonder* grins beatifically at last,

a *hasty* guillotine of white whale teeth gnash,

he *boasts*, "The coast can be claimed *new* land this fast!"

He wakes to snarling whales *heard* under the bed,

from coffee cup, mother's *lies*, what the doctor said.

3

His mind swims laps around Starbuck's *state* skull,

adrenalin pools in *time's* dive fathoms deep,

leg tangled harpoon *hate*, rope thrown smash cruel,

awaits the snap *gathered* in the whale's dragged down sleep.

No *fortune's* captive *accident* dream mystery,

enthralled with discontent he swims up the *Thames*

through each thread of liquid *fashioned* tapestry

where what's first *dyed for goodness* next bleaches hymns.

The most incomprehensible *politic* tales

of a universe *unfathered*, Einstein muttered

as *heretic policy* rode atomic whales,

witnessed its wonders comprehensibly *numbered*.

At *Time's* gravity mixer, *hours* stir & shake

pulled bloody spears from the *drowned* heart of Moby Dick.

[Epiphany Crown for Bob Dylan's Noble Prize]

for Martin Jenkins

Big Bang Nutshell Time

1 Stephen Hawking's M-theory of Everything

Unfolding soul shrouds extra dimension access,

awaits our optical solution equations,

set problems calculate artificial success,

held currents move in law compactifications.

Passed depth, height, width, time's six other dimensions stand,

accounts level out the multiverse playing field,

compactified planet staged in a grain of sand

unnoticeable in infinite space-time yield.

Like trachyons appear first as shadow before light,

colliding particles, string theory graviton

moves double gravity while pulsing beyond sight

with particle super-partner symmetry on.

Nutshell Big Bang cellular twist-folds merge as one,

as pairs of eyes do always on some horizon,

2 Redundant Pyramids: Cydonia / Cairo

Crop circles fold tetrahedrons' Merkaba field,

19.5 degrees of latitude displays

Cydonia Martian sphinx face's attitude yield,

designs of extraterrestrial grand arrays.

The pareidolia gaze on Orion's Belt,

exact alignment with Giza pyramid tops,

Cydonia pyramid ruins, Martian melt

of structures conform to Golden Mean space-time spots.

Embedded patterns of Gaia's sacred lights,

"Earth's Grid," Hugh Newman found, 19.5 degrees,

conforms to add hyper dimensional sites,

light's chariot of macro / micro God decrees.

Al–Qahirah, Cairo, "Mars the victorious,"

Egyptians saw Mars as horizon sky's Horus.

3 Galactic Origami Soul

Brain surface grows folds from its core to inner sight

the way tri-horn beetle wings unfold then seek flight.

The Big Bang gravities gather dark matter turns

from micro to macro repeating patterns.

Amino acids, 20, to multitude bones,

attack disease with protein keys, unlock control,

DNA unfolds genetic Rosetta Stones

on cellular levels, origami of soul.

Love's gesture in a nutshell with oyster pearl eye

reflects a blood wolf moon like a scab in the sky

contracts a sign of doom's eclipse emersion,

eclipses double helix entangled vision,

the starlings' murmuration origami cloud

caught up portending a galactic throbbing shroud.

The nut-shelled Big Bang's cellular twist-fold explodes,

a hexagram sequence of souls turns what unfolds.

Lux Volupté's Calm Matisse Harbor

Society plays *living's vein* of *grace,*

lux time notes press, voluptuous space *laced* refrains,

proud lively tunes, a multitude of *lives* in peace...

the lyre *paints nature's infectious* rhythmic *gains.*

One *day* composed from everyday *now* closed,

love's harbor over laid shimmer of *rosiness,*

rewards *she stored* in the rich shiny posed

reflected *blushing* frets, nude sunset bliss.

What she doesn't *steal* from lightning's electric cry,

impiety chimes as the thirteenth of never,

moon's constant *shadowed* face returns the answer why

advantages in each *hue should live* forever.

Her naked *beauty's presence imitates* the *rose,*

bleeds twilight's ultraviolet calm rainbows...

Mother's Spirit (63)

They each took turns & curled *against* her side

as she lay on her last bed's *time* to fly,

her sons & daughters, one by one *fortified*

by her goodness, their goodness to *fortify*

as she lay *vanishing* to take the sky

to welcome *beauty's* liberated spirit,

receive her *travel* well to shrouded cloud's bright eye,

embraced with *age*, her sacred *King* to clear it.

A soul's *sweet* child returned to her children

from end to end, *love's* unending *sight* that bends

back through them over *memory* back again,

as steady, *never cut*, what *love* contends.

You'll want her there in your last *hour's* descent,

to brush the *lines & wrinkles* out, shake up ascent.

for Guy Charleville

82

A Sect of One (*Plus One*)   (143)

Lo, hoped for human muse, mentor the *mothered* gun

your life had stood, a harbinger *creature's* touchstone,

a talisman's *reprise*, Jung's *running* "sect of one,"

her words *cried* sermons, transcendental Dickinson.

Inclusion in a double-*catch dispatch* with *you,*

to know *you* in the carriage *pursuit* next *to me,*

two couplets *hold your neglected* garden in view,

the horse heads neigh *bent* to *face* the oak & posy.

The circled coming *stay,* forever *busy* full,

entirely for Shakespeare, *crying* in constraints,

where revelations *chase,* ours *fly* the *back turned* tool,

behold *me,* next to *you, kiss me,* one of *your* saints.

To stanza-land we hurry, *pray* for *Will's* same *care,*

your bearings *catch* us in the breathless *turn,* Walt's share.

This antique book *returns* to great psalm's grace

when *bent* to each one, ambient to each ones place

as written in the quick of a *catching* heart,

not far *behind* words *prayed* to *quicken* future art.

The *child-like* hand that curved a holy specter's mind,

two points' perspective into the future shined.

Whether troubadour's *loud* warble or David's tale

unbound to *chase* the secret in the thunder's bell,

until the shepherd's flock through new madrigals *fly*,

embrace her *housewife cares, kind face* with kindest eye.

1 Quantum Entanglement

If *seeing* it changes it, when is it real

or *broken* in a throw of quantum dice?

Two people separate, distance identical,

one particle influences the other, *twice*...

same *constancy* travels faster than light,

unlimited *blindness,* then to reappear,

the same equation's *enlightenment* right,

a quantum point *bearing* access right here...

We *vowed* in the same world's symmetrical bell

that rang through Germany's *foresworn* classroom door,

till I arrived *unknown* at her White Sands neighbor

years later... again, Susan's *truth* wed me to tell...

a Tao of parallels in the physics of *things*,

remotely *sworn* for future, quantum's system clings...

Truth reaffirms change, psyche's regeneration,

unmasked *faith-torn* trial's haunted generation.

2 Heavenly Dream World: First Level

Susan's *faith* rewound, resurrection Sabbath morn

after three days, *honest* dream, Guy's visitation,

her busy *bearing*, our *new* house separation,

had to ask how she liked it, to check scorn once *sworn*.

Among her beautiful *loved things* not to forget,

Guy's *truth* smiled from his resurrected body

& *loved* us with a baby elephant pet,

artful on the sofa so we'd rub its belly.

Then Guy & I walked on paths by fields *vowing* wheat,

to steep high footbridge, a *deep* stream under our feet

led to schoolyard cheer, *enlightened* students to greet,

new classroom windows large streamed wisdom's *kind* retreat.

Truth reaffirmed change, psyche's regeneration,

unmasked *faith-torn* trial's haunted generation.

3 Her Next Life Visitation

Framed dreams lined up like *vowed* series of thoughts

bearing layers, departing, *new* destinations,

degrees of parted *loved* ones, couldn't & could knots,

in *honest* labyrinths, sequenced tabulations.

Deep oath as married, once divorced, in after death

unaltered *love* light's constant justification,

before death's *act* sorts truer kinds of breath,

black void *breached* to *new* visionary union.

The angels *know* we'll peer to search light's dark region,

enlightened work to the fielded dream's completion;

beside the counter, tall bookshelves, *kind* perfect wife

stands, unconditional *love's* resurrected life!

Truth reaffirms change, psyche's regeneration,

unmasked *faith-torn* trial's haunted generation.

for Guy & Susan

Yeats' Last Paradigm Vision

They lay in love, that first day of new sun,

had seen each other once in one day's dawn,

her face, something of sun, held everyone

enthralled to poetry, no need be drawn

for image making, so-and-so would come

to populate with ease of garden birth,

where all but one fruit's never cumbersome,

ecstatic copulations, steady mirth!

No shriven courtesy, love's holograph,

no need to read, quote/unquote learned books,

as nothing idle, all shines free enough.

Colloquial stars, invitation looks

contained raptures, diametrical tunes,

each celebrated phases of new moons.

Her Unburdened Prescience   (65)

Her spirit writes the better part of her *power*

consuming light, her words long *mortal* composure,

the other side of sleep, *beauty* waking over

dreams flowing shades deep, double *wracked* exposure.

The dual *day*, word-winded *restful* prescient breath,

like smoke rises, a *honey* consciousness incense.

Her words refuse *impregnable* ravages, death,

with montage eye, rye rabbi, suspense *black ink* sense.

Her poems, a mother's well prepared *jeweled* nest,

for milking kindness nurtured *time-chest* waterlines.

Her eyes shined *meditation's* philosopher test,

wisdom's gemstones of eternal *miracle* signs.

Unburdened by death, lines dig, *decay*, exhume,

replant the love of her words, *shine bright* to full bloom.

for Maxine Cassin

89

Lin Emery Circle's Cursive Flight   (108)

Flight's orbital edge wings its *figured* lives,

rotating sky fins like wielding *spirit* knives,

a shrine's *divine* suspense for palm, lily pad pond,

carves dragonfly mist, turns banana's *hallowed* frond.

The arch in the oak limb curves to *count* a star,

presages lunar half-*days* from where we are.

Flight's *prayer* to magnolia bloom, lotus blossom,

to balance eagle wing, *antiquity* contained,

flies future's *wrinkle* through fluid aluminum,

the *character* of wind's eclipse attained.

The wingtip dips invisible *ink* to eye,

imaginary flight in *place* to augur sky

where birds can not fly & *dust* gather inside,

the nest of intuitive landing *weighs* to glide,

a *page's* span, word, phrase, sentence, mission,

expressive action symbol, way of word fission.

Hunched over Notre Dame

The hand made nun's wax spills as covered with his blood,

don't get too close to her gold sling-shot crucifix,

no match lit in the candle shop fire flood,

live wire sparks behind her wall that starts to hiss.

The steeple in a cloud stood upright stout,

above cathedral billows, altar, turned, fell down...

did Jesus framed in rafters just then shout,

grime faced in cubist vestments, neck bent to look out?

No need for crown of thorns, roof nails impaled the same,

a sudden moment shaken down from Notre Dame

held madness, French ladies could not avert their gaze,

turn iPhones from their sad cathedral wrapped in flames.

Good Friday's silenced bell can't rescue what it lacks,

the rafters must be climbed pressed against their hunched backs.

Firefighters stand the blaze crack rumbled thunder,

as thousands of bees still buzz the rooftop beehive,

& billionaires speed to rebuild wages, wonder

how Yellow Jackets on Champs-Élysée survive.

Celestial Accounting with Cubits (148)

Arch pointed, vaulted ceiling, *fault's* flying buttress,

counts faith that built the *fled world's* gothic cathedral.

From sacred numbers God *denotes* the multiverse

& building heaven's *corresponding* vehicle.

The cubit, from elbow to *judgment's* finger tip,

wide 50 cubits, Noah's *cunning* rainbow arc,

then 30, 60, Solomon's *eyed* temple strip,

oraculorum's *censure* cubit measured mark.

What need have we to measure the city *falsely*,

top 144 cubit *watching* walls,

without the wrestled angel ladder's *viewed* pity,

to paradise through doors down *true sight's* halls,

to *marvel* galaxies like Meadowlark Lemon,

till heaven's dome *clears* steps ahead as counted down?

Delicate Thunder Embraced Awareness

Delicate thunder softly overwhelmed my ear's

torment, as recollection's amen-corner of

my meditation alignment with what it hears,

distilled scenes, punctuated revelation love.

The next world she'll live better lived in beyond

among attending spirits of the thunder dome

who weigh belled better judgments, little prayers fond,

resounding to hearts deceitful, crooked, rung home.

What justice prevails when her friend's blithe Iago

works rendered Othello's last pillow ordered thrown,

as if the two bad daughters of Lear's overthrow

capitulated clutched kingdom theft's last agon?

The spirits hear me contemplate the action's ends,

with thunder emphasize my phrased accounts of friends.

Apocalyptic Cycle

Thank you for keeping all my truths bound up to wrap,

it caused the questioning of everything till tapped,

how feet move freely without fear of bones that snap

against a floor of concrete sealed deceits entrapped.

The visionary dreams unchosen by reason,

truth's due given extremes to measured remedy,

time's weathered personal wear, shared each ones season,

divined to match in other books what's meant to be.

As rituals search out a rightful proving ground,

the reborn visit's glory appeared fully formed

of unconditional love, perfect, no one scorned,

did not view every rite, in fullness stood reformed

with special care for each one's undistracted scope,

contrived dreams carry now more varied doors of hope

to destinations hurried, the same dual goal,

where laid up treasure expounds on homes of renewed soul.

Guy's Revivified Mind

With Guy there was never an unresolved conflict,

his lead example cushioned falling hard knocks,

passed on his nature's open space to connect

with those at odds, how some recalcitrant child talks.

My spots of time with Guy return to every plight

of lifted edges he saw through under each rock

that troubled other teachers' less budging insight.

Guy gave to hapless violent souls kindness to shock

complacency from change if slammed against a wall.

The smiling hands-on approach Guy shares with his wife,

stayed passed on to a friend & kindly led the call,

all hiking to the mountains, renews the good life.

I look toward tough times when thoughts on Guy so kind

with Janice, Vivian, revivify my mind.

Credit where Credit's Due

Discovering faced books online a bit late,

you've heard it, better late than disavowed fate,

better turns to your hegemonic state,

hedged up so fast it doesn't need a past due date

when your future's all thumbs up right here & now,

a great hitch-hiker riding a cosmic tail-gate,

all thumbs one day, then declensions the great debate,

your word *abomination* ..sums up the planned how

deep you strive for presence, to be on the right side,

cast horse-race bet ramifications, do or try,

until they catch up with you, find how to decide

what stretches reason's stance, you teach how to cry.

Your cause as big as Ben Bernanke's saves the world,

at last credit counseling put out fires hurled.

Angel Trumpets

1 All for your Everything   (85)

Will you have my all for your *tongue-tied* everything,

convince your skeptic turn *compiled* to ride me out

where nature churns the *reserved* stomach's muscling

in on receiving *precious* signals from the gut?

We were acquainted first through the same *muse's* friends,

returned to *hymns* a *lettered* intimate season.

Determined break from *clerks* on which my *pen* depends,

caused *polished* choice to reconsider chosen.

Few carry me away *hearing* the way you do,

the hunting in your eye still *praises* my twilight,

astonished cares prepared to know this *love for you*,

your *hindsight's* dangerous dark rooms at midnight.

Break through tomorrow's Roman holiday *respects*,

high mission morning's impossible way *effects*.

2 Time Heals, Wounds to Heal (86)

Time takes the distillation of its *proud* effects

to new *bound* depths poured through a precious past,

night's undertow that falls with *rehearsed* affects,

shrunk present moving upstream, *verse entombed* at last.

Time's not Love's fool, hands cannot clutch *spirit* seconds

then envy loss, her captive *mortal* numbered face.

Tell love a thing or two of *night's* demanding ends

beyond the watchman's *lines* calling out dawn's burnt pace,

bound up clocks speared by shaken *ghostly* times,

each day's half-cut worn *nightly* weathered blue surprise.

The hungered *victor's* beaten counts of hollow crimes,

rewound spring *fears*, self-wounds *sickness* personifies.

The clock-face world *filled*, every *lifeline* unwound

as hours pass, unwinds what *matters*, heals the wound.

3 Spirit Guide   (87)

Consuming life's last quadrant, *farewell's* last wound,

to Simon's Rome, *charter* Dr. Bloom as Virgil,

set up discovery *bonds*, pass exiled contents bound.

Feed deep on *granted* forces waiting in the Grail,

mine caves for *riches*, noble canon fodder,

explode *sleep* darkness with *determining* art,

aligned to *swerve* Galileo's alma mater,

illuminating navigation's *knowing* chart.

Perceived at times more clearly *given* bright in *dreams*,

imagination *misprision* fired, heaven slakes,

quenched where extended *better judgment* teems.

With shadowed faces, *estimate* their marks...

when hewing mind's eye, *knowing's* canonical

possessing heresy's *waking* gnostic temple.

4 Incarnadine Mind   (88)

Time's sprung, *disposed* in a blossomed rose-wound temple,

encrypted springs to *merit* first selected leads,

their diagram, DNA's *vantage* point *double*,

proves *bending* moon's eclipse corona bleeds

out curving edges, *set* rose-gold, haloes circle,

dual wheels inner *gain* for second crown's sharper thorns,

twined *virtuous* vined helix, geared cyclical

to *injured* going of a Fisher King's returns.

A Passover sunset's *scornful* golden aspect,

incarnadine pearl mother's *love-light* horizon

on *tainted* moon's first shell, pink pearl cloud duet,

low galleon cloud leans, *concealed* tether to sun.

The lake soon *parts* a *losing* skyline blotted dark,

the *eye of storm*, moon as earth's *forsworn* ark.

5 Divined Family   (89)

Where Dante's exile *forsakes* Beatrice' arc,

hears Solomon's song *defend* newer testament,

his *tongue* no longer *reasoned* artifice as dark,

new wine's *acquaintance* flask, old skin shed sacrament.

She *loves* the *will* of messianic vision,

rose blossomed mindful mother's *beloved* peace

from ages *old* where middle age looks on

as *loved ones dwell* where futures *will* not cease.

When entering tomorrow's *desired* rest

between the covering wings to *tell* ark angels,

her *name* beatified curves out his *form* the best,

resets the bonds sustaining *debated* angles.

Was better he'd been born *vowed* to be exiled,

than ever see her *hating* her imperfect child.

6 Great Catch   (90)

His loaves served the *windswept world's* wayward child,

rain stopper, lake walker, bread basket diplomat,

across set tables *woeful* enemies schemed wild,

he fished for fishers, future *fortune's* habitat.

Three days of anguish swallowed *loss* like Jonah's shock,

escaped to beach with friends & feast on *fortune's* fish,

spared *grief's spite*, *left* with interstellar Enoch,

to build their parallel mansions, *strain* planned anguish.

When whale oil *last* stretched *nights* in the temple lamp,

the *worst* of light was veiled, *lingered* for the Romans

whose siege below *conquered* walls would not break camp

until cursed stones *came down* to fill omens.

The woman at his *deeds* last supper broke bread,

compared first counted loaves & fish debris point spread.

7 Body's Heir (91)

Some glory in manifesting destiny's spread,

poetic long *skills*, primed subversive ends,

when heard what curse to move his bone's *rest* would be said,

the broken stones fit back where *adjunct* work contends.

Control the stomach to *garment* the soul

like Parsifal's quest fielding new green *richer* corn,

the *body*, spirit, mind, *alone*, *wealth* of the whole,

to be as *measured*, born for *body's force* reborn.

Attentive rings rhymed of a *general* sonneteer,

yields *humor's* echo, *proud love's* thorough *bettered* year,

finds life's short lease fitted for *higher* views,

returns remembrance of cost, *pleasured* dues.

Well tempered with *new-fangled ill's* glad sorrowing,

will you have my *all* for your tongue-tied everything?

ASAP: Age of Second Adam's Paradigm

The wings of birds in flight, the ideal smile
of Leonardo's resurrected pointing John,
the finger painted Mona's, never out of style,
reveals self-knowledge, deflects ones prison archon.
Preparing for the final conflict's cosmic seam,
Blue Turbaned Prince, Persian devouring Beast,
twilight adjacent time, twixt waking thought & dream,
angelic blessing for the coming written feast...
A six-string medley of three songs cascade,
to tall oaks as their inner flight rose in song,
a choir of birds chime flourishes to chiming played,
a sect of one's oracle lifts the song along.
Passed winged words parting on a razor's edge
while contemplating angels from a mountain ledge
who travel deep in valleys for a second look
between the pages fading of a mission book,
the end returns Pleroma's unfallen fullness,
to find us resting there in perpetual bliss.

Under the Orbital Lilac Tree

Between the lines' material, chasing the moon

his Kosmos calls from an orbital lilac tree,

its taproot tallying the orbs of destiny

as I lie in glowing fields, dream up his night's tune.

To watch him gaze at stars, the same wrapt everything,

no old man here from timeless aspirations fled,

his daylight transcendental smile, Kosmic thinking

eclipses earth with other moons where death has sped

like night-birds to her virtue's inward sunshine eye,

content perfection's inherited grace

as sudden ease of focus pulls love in to fly

desire's sweetest lines, drawn to her sovereign face.

Why would love happen not at death's call of beauty?

There'll be no "no's" for you not to know no pity.

A Unified Field Ballad

To touch fingers of nature's hidden hand

spells out in numerological laws,

the warp & weft of sky relative to land

& how ground gravitates in space-time's clause.

Why does the hydrogen atom not radiate

like Mercury spinning around the sun,

as geometry's warps & curves calculate

the ever accelerating creation?

The black hole error turned against curvature

within blackout moonstone's sarcophagus roll,

stone tossed ripple's mathematical architecture

shows up lastly where time elapsed, to slower soul,

the great equation of unification,

eternity's passed future enumeration...

Appendix

Fields of Dreams: Symbols of Consciousness

As "Leaves of Grass," Walt Whitman named his expanding book with a metaphorical and allusive title. "Leaves," pages of his poems, stretches from noun to verb for how grass grows and withers in a cycle of nature, appearing then leaving, then reappearing, etc. The noun-verb alludes to four Psalms (37:2, 90:5-6, 103:15, 102:4) and several New Testament passages with the grass metaphor on the nature of human life. One may Google for proof of his title's transcendental aspect. Although more thorough at times than the mind, there is no artificial consciousness in Google.

Dr. Harold Bloom in the *Leaves of Grass,* 150th anniversary 1[st ed.] reprint intro, refers to the "Whitman sublime" being unsurpassed among modern English language poets with only Emily Dickinson coming close (p. xvi). Dr. Bloom identifies the "paradigm" of Whitman's sublime as the *King James Bible* with Walt's essential poetics marked by the translations of William Tyndale and Miles Coverdale (p. xxii). He goes on to examine where Walt's Americansensibilities were filtered through the transcendental lens of Ralph W. Emerson's essays such as: *The Over-Soul*; *Spiritual Laws* and *The Poet*, as if Whitman reflected Emerson's major ideas that ignited imagination. If Walt's sublime as individual prophet of a new American love religion issued from Emerson's harbinger prose, Dr. Bloom finds it in the essays where Emerson calls on the "method-men" as "symbols of consciousness" (p. xxiii). This is what resonates with Whitman to fill the "poet-void" Emerson describes in *The Poet*.

Google's artificial intelligence, not consciousness, searches unlike autonomous self-driving cars, as that skillset's current jargon uses a new word, "roadmanship," based on driver road safety measures, according to *Wired* magazine (3/2019 p. 19). The same *Wired* issue, the essay, *Alexa, I want Answers*, by James Vlahos (p. 59) on "voice computing," shares challenges seeking "the one perfect response to any question" from how answers may rank upwardly on the knowledge response chain. This leads to imagine new word creations like "truthmanship," "questmanship," etc. A closer step toward Star Trek suggests "Scotty, beam me the answer."

The voice-computing article opens and closes with thoughts on the work of William Tunstall-Pedoe, who created what led to the Echo & "Alexa" and how after leaving Amazon in 2016, he "acknowledges that voice oracles introduce new risks, or at least worsen existing ones" …these problems can be solved by "better technology… AIs that learn to suppress factually incorrect info" (p. 67) …perhaps in a way that his software, Anagram Genius, helped Dan Brown " generate "plot-critical puzzles" in *The Da Vinci Code* (p. 61).

A correctness measure may one day be called "truthmanship" in bearing artificially intelligent research across media applications. The word could apply to human thought processes and the outcome of reasoning in how Vlahos (p. 61) says "Search engines as helpful librarians… must eventually yield to AIs as omniscient oracles." As verification measures are applied to truth in various digital media accounts, a current contention, to near paranoia, is suggested by Zeynep Tufekci in the *Wired* issue (p. 19): "Every verification method carries the threat of surveillance."

When self-directed surveillance involves a transcendentalist poet like Whitman, engaged in his era's journalism for several years, as a reader of the classics and serious contemporaries such as Emerson, the efforts resulted in poems like "Song of Myself" and the entire scope of *Leaves of Grass*. Ezra Pound surveyed it as having "one sap and one root" with him, though it was Walt who, he wrote, had "broke the new wood" of which Pound wanted "carving" and shared "commerce."

Would it seem odd to Professor Bloom who deemed Emerson "our John the Baptist" with Walt "certainly the American literary Christ" (L/G intro p. xxxiii) to find me considering Walt's Psalm allusions in what may be one of the most non-paranoid grand poetics ever written in English?

The self-surveillance in *Leaves of Grass* may also remind one of a New Testament story (John 1: 45-49) (not to take considerations away from the Gnostic *Gospel of Thomas*.) When Philip told Nathanael who had not yet met Jesus that here was the one the old prophets wrote of, Nathanael asked if anything good could come out of Nazareth. Upon meeting, Jesus declared him a true Israelite in whom there is no guile, to which Nathanael asked how did he know him. Jesus related that he observed Nathanael under a fig tree before Philip found him, apparently without the knowledge of those there, to which Nathanael exclaimed verification of Jesus as King of Israel and his Lord. The observation amounts to surveillance Nathanael sees as non-threatening or could it be good-threatening? Jesus then tells Nathanael he shall see greater things such as heaven open and angels ascending and descending. Could what happened under the fig tree have something to do with an angel? It does not say, but sensibilities are heightened due to compact details engaged in "truthmanship" that sets up faith in what is not yet seen based on former surveillance.

There is little doubt that Walt Whitman understood deep useful intelligence was rooted in an attitude of faith and earned through experience. The appearance of idleness and glorious hard physical work, this dual attitude, is presented as the front print in *Leaves of Grass* by Whitman's stance, right fist on hip tilt, left hand in pants pocket, head tilt, hat cocked to the side, relaxed man of action, seriously gazing at the viewer to come to grips with truth.

110

The trilogy, *Shakespeare AI*, took shape from sonnet forms with rules of content and container to become a vehicle for expressions of life mysteries. A writer friend challenged me to write sonnets and others encouraged continuing them. There have been writer friends who belittled the idea at best and even mocked or ridiculed the notion, implying that while perhaps conversing with Shakespeare, it had no relevance to them or current serious writing in our time, being as obsolete as a useless antique. Nevertheless, I built a book of sonnets allowed to multiply, divide and change over 15 years that involved essay and letter writing before coming to its own completion.. not knowing this last expanse of writing would involve the shocking deaths of Guy Charleville, a dearest teacher co-worker friend and my beloved Susan, librarian ex-wife. I had hoped the book would somehow help absolve me in her eyes.

As expected, after their deaths in less than a month, Dec. 21, 2018 his, and hers, Jan. 12, 2019, a series of dreams came, followed by poems and the realization that the reactions to these poems and dreams through an exchange of letters with my theatrical singer friend, Diana, who two years prior had lost her husband, Wesley, spurred the need to write. The new poems give the book a more profound completion in a planned 4th volume, *Radio Waves for the Blind*. YouTube video interviews on life after death with hypnotherapist Dolores Cannon, shared comparable dream events in line with some experiences in the trilogy. There remain things she accepted in her broad range of "truthmanship" after working for 40 years regressing clients through passed lives as subconscious conduits to spirit realm personalities working out karma issues, I clearly can not yet abide with.

Volume 1, *Shakespeare's Wake*, began and resolved with dreams; 1st: a night's angelic visitation, while in bed seeming to be dreamily awake, aware of the room and lying there, feet toward the window, she end's up placing my resting left hand on my heart as if to quickly consecrate a writer; 2: In an epilogue poem, my adopting army dad appeared wonderfully in another most lucid realistic dream. The poem *Resurrection Visitation* expands on it with Shakespeare sonnet (151) allusions:

"*Content* internal radiance like fire baptized,
  he left *me* waking to *his* death defect as *prized*."

An awesome blessing, its joyous seriousness spread curious delight, calm in afterlife observations among diverse people in a new/old city. The reunion, visited by dad as my guide from an army clapboard clinic door, on a ramp to a huge grand old brownstone busy church-like porch. He stepped down smiling to greet my awe and show me among fine youthful men and women, another similar brownstone, letting me enter, look around see its surface renovation work in the entry room, kind men working calmly, then in an empty fine hall leading to rooms where I alone, not yet prepared to go, chose to return to him on the sidewalk. He left, no look back, bounded up the stairs in his perfect green fatigues and boots, to a new porch and gently slipped through the partially opened door, ending the dream.

Volume two, *Recycling the Circle*, deals with social, political, cultural, psychological, scientific and philosophical modern issues and contains as many prints as poems. While structuring and formatting material the death of Stephen Hawking happened from which an extended sonnet came. This gave the book an ending relative to some advanced scientific thought and physics jargon of the day.

It opens with a sonnet on the idea of Dr. Martin Luther King Jr. and Abraham Lincoln sharing a double memorial. A sonnet competing with a monument was proposed by Shakespeare in his Sonnet 55. Two sonnets and more later enlarged the series for a chapbook. In one sonnet sequence, *Redundant Pyramids*, pertains to Martian forms aligned in relation to pyramids of Giza and Orion star groupings. The third sonnet of this "epiphany crown," *Galactic Origami Soul*, blends modern science with organically mystical nature myths of the soul. The volume 2 cover has Lin Emery's *Flight* sculpture replacing Lee on the monument as in a dream in 2000 and remembered when arriving at Lee Circle that morning while driving Susan to work at the main library. I returned to take photos and plan double exposures to explore the dream at length, over several months, many rolls of film and lots of sketches. Gradually a series of prints added to the B&W volume 2 and became a plan for a large format color edition.

Volume three, *Romance Languages*, started as a comedic parody on the muses Shakespeare frequently engaged with in his sonnets. It has a composite picture of Susan from behind at a Mardi Gras float raising her hands to catch a Rex throw on Canal Street in the late 90's. The cover collage title is *Grasping the Unattainable*. Most of the illustrations in the current set up are elegant parodies of Leonardo da Vinci's main depicted ladies in drawings and paintings, all with wine glasses, at Stonehenge for the "First Picnic" which is also intended as a satire of Dan Brown's book, *The Da Vinci Code*. Monty Python's Terry Gilliam was also a bit influential.

On her condo couch, I showed Susan different versions of the volumes with illustrations. It was her first evening out of the hospital after chemo and radiation therapy was completed and the same day, but we did not know then, that Guy was killed in a car wreck as a passenger in his own Honda Civic, the same death trap car, as I've heard it called, that was owned by Susan.

Susan's condition deteriorated in the next few days with low blood pressure and dehydration to the point where the doctor ordered her return. Her friend Tony called on the morning of Jan. 12 and said Susan was rushed from a nursing home recovery to the emergency room with chest pains where she was pronounced dead. On Jan. 14th I received a card from Janice, Guy's wife, thanking me for the trilogy where she found the poem written for Guy on the death of his mother, she wrote she would keep it and me close to her heart.

Two nights before Susan died, *Einstein's Quantum Riddle* was shown on PBS, a vivid dream followed with Susan and Guy that helped stop my bedtime weeping for a while. More expected dreams came that were noted while researching several books, the internet, YouTube videos and while writing two "epiphany crowns." *Haunted Generation 2*, fit the trilogy's expanded ending as *Big Bang Nutshell Time* fleshed out volume two's ending. Altogether the series held plans for a chapbook sequence.

Guy and Susan looked their best in the dreams ..no words recalled, they seemed delighted being there. Susan in her pre-death dream looked superb in casual elegant light pastel pants and long sleeved top in our stately white two story New Orleans manor with shiny cherry-rosewood floors, cream walls, with soft accented shadows in corners. Clear amber tinged light streamed through an open window's white sheer breezy curtains at the far side of the spacious living room, while bright outside from other angles. Verbally subdued, busy with beautiful household objects and modern furniture, moving from the kitchen, as a cat wandered by to other rooms, Susan didn't pay much attention to me. I had to ask how she liked this place, implied as compared to the previous places we lived in that she didn't care much for. She showed her interest as if it were a rhetorical question, obvious to see, while she kept busy turned to fine new things with no conversation.

Guy rounded the driveway by a tall hedge and nicely edged grassy front yard, dressed in a dapper deep olive/green hiking outfit. I met him dressed as usual, neat Ralph Lauren Polo double pocket dark shirt and tan chinos as on beautiful days when we taught middle school Special Ed. boys and girls at Eisenhower Elementary. He was happy to greet me, as if after a long journey, returned from a great distance. Going inside to see Susan and the house, we checked out three sweet cats, then Guy suddenly surprised us in the living room from a hallway with a baby pet elephant that acted like a big puppy climbing on a chair then rolled around next on the sofa for a belly rub. This playful greeting was a lot of fun for all of us. After that Guy and I went out a side patio door to a grassy yard and walked to a lane by rows of fine two story houses, then a field by a stream with a high footbridge, down to houses before a newly renovated high tech industrial building for a school on the neighborhood outskirts by fields.

113

Arriving at the site we met a group of delightfully eager middle school students in the yard. They lined up casually, chatting while waiting to enter the building. Guy and I entered a side door on a wide hall that led to our new large well-appointed classroom with tables, computers and film screen. Huge windows let enough light in to make the open space look luminous and transparent throughout. A small group of girls and boys sat at a side table as Guy began casually discussing the day's nature/space science study. I planned visual media and art supplies for the subject while observing them. All were delighted to be there for this learning reunion as if every day from then on would be "Happy Earthday" in and beyond school.

After waking from the dream there came a sense of relief about Guy, just as when dad appeared in the dream revealing his revitalized new life after death as we know it, to graciously share a welcoming glimpse of this glorious new state.

My long time actor, filmmaker, singer, talent-teacher friend Diana, had commented on the first improved version of the book I gifted her. She found large parts of it difficult to comprehend and realized its tedious task to complete. She wanted to help with the book by generously offering to pass it on to her editor uncle. It needed work on continued updates and improvements before someone tried to wrap a mind around it.

While musing on the similarities and contrasts of poems with documentary films, my friend Paulette sent a link to the critic Roger Ebert's essay on Werner Herzog films that linked to an interview with Herzog. Roger said, "He is willing to push beyond documentary fact... in his quest for underlying truth Herzog moves freely through spheres of fact, fiction, legend, myth and invention." At the Telluride interview with Roger on Sept. 29, 1998, Werner said, "Theweakness of cinema verite' documentaries is that they can not go any deeper. They can only reach the surface of what constitutes truth in cinema. Deeper truth can only be found in poetry, because then you start to fabricate. The world is simply there. It is what men find in it and bring to it that is truth. I am in search of the fathomless." Roger wrapped it up with, "It takes art, the arranging and adjusting, to fashion someone else's experience into our own."

I thought of Diana's quest to complete her documentary after Wesley's death two years earlier and wondered how much these ideas figured into her efforts. She read my new poems that came as I began to process the deaths of Guy and Susan. It was touching and illuminating to get her feedback. She intuitively wanted to clarify my efforts and help by considering the epiphany crown's first of three sonnets word for word and line by line.

The time-saddled methods of the process, allowing the poem, and book, to show how to proceed over time required subconscious and conscious links to visualize what leads to completion. Links, like allusions, a conduit for magination, play a crucial role in the work's development. Language use was for an enrichment of imaginative experience in trusting the higher reaches of subconscious mind while at times recognizing when dipping into the pool of universal unconscious mind. The mind should be allowed to wander, even fail as Jeff Bezos, among others, has said in group motivational meetings.

After awhile Diana responded with a detailed account of parsing the first poem for meaning and asked for clarifications in the following relaxed, non-critical, complementary way.. here is the poem revised a bit first:

Haunted Generation 2 (Shakespeare Sonnet 152 allusions in italics)

1 Quantum Entanglement

If *seeing* it changes it, when is it real

or *broken* in a throw of quantum dice?

Two people separate, distance identical,

one particle influences the other, *twice*…

same *constancy* travels faster than light,

unlimited *blindness,* then to reappear,

the same equation's *enlightenment* right,

a quantum point *bearing* access right here…

We *vowed* in the same world's symmetrical bell

that rang through Germany's *foresworn* classroom door,

till I arrived *unknown* at her White Sands neighbor

years later... again, Susan's *truth* wed me to tell…

a Tao of parallels in the physics of *things*,

remotely *sworn* for future, quantum's system clings…

Truth reaffirms change, psyche's regeneration,

unmasked *faith-torn* trial's haunted generation.

In reading this Haunted Generation 2 - I really liked it.

As I don't know what everything means, I wrote down what I believe

you mean and ask for clarification. Thanks.

So for fun and as a challenge to me, tell me how close am I

to understanding. Haunted Generation: (Sins of our families, fathers,

that carry down from generation to generation)

If seeing it changes it, when is it real - I Love this!

Dictionary defines Quantum as any of the very small increments or

parcels into which many forms of energy are subdivided" and dice as:

a gambling game played. Can you - for clarification please, tell me

what you mean by "broken in a throw of quantum dice

Two people separate, distance identical - (I love this!)

unlimited blindness then to reappear, (This means both parties continue

to not "see" –each other, or their relationship, the others' needs, etc

116

One particle influences the other, (love this) twice

Same constancy travels faster than light, (The constancy of what?)

"Unlimited blindness then to reappear, (love this)

the same equation's enlightenment right, " (What does this mean to you,

please?" a quantum bearing accessed as right here... (an increment

providing an opening?) She and I vowed in the symmetrical bell ringing

in Germany's foresworn classroom. (You met in Germany, at school,

and married to the ringing of wedding bells)

arriving at her White Sands unknown neighbor's home (White Sands, a

town, and "unknown neighbor's home," someone who lived near by and

she didn't know them years later, late again, Susan's truth out to tell...

a Tao of parallels in universal things. (timing was off, yet Susan speaks

her truth and opinions of general life matters.) remotely sworn for future

(Things she vowed to continue to share years

earlier) quantum's system cling's (?) Truth reaffirms change,

psyche's regeneration, (thus, the "Entanglement")

unmasked fear- (love this) torn trial's haunted generation. (the haunted

legacy left after life's trials torn by courage to face and show one's fear.

The poet John Keats came to a concept like an attitude he named as "Negative Capability" that could stimulate expansion of consciousness for the imagination considering poetic constructs. In a letter to a friend he said the idea worked as a literary ingredient, an attitude of acceptability to "be in doubts and ambiguities" for a deeper imaginative experience of poetry than just the surface intentions of literal meaning. Keats mentioned Shakespeare possessed large quantities of Negative Capability throughout the plays, including the sonnets, which reveals and needs a reader's "tour de force" of Negative Capability to fully engage the imagination.

Here begins the parsing of Diana's parsing: her last statement resonates the most imaginative experience, "life's trials torn by courage" where she tries to parse the title "Haunted Generation," while not "seeing" psychological layers of experience reflected by "2." A "haunting" can be involuntary returns, something generated" as a caused experience and can be cyclical in a "generational" aspect.

Part 1, *Quantum Entanglement*, is a physics concept unseen to the naked-eye based on scientific equations, post-event observation or conjectured activity with a theory of quantum particles, so small the thing is "there but not there" to perception where the observation itself effects it. This mysterious event, like briefly glimpsed symbols moving in a minute (yet vast) scaled atomic universe, another symmetrical aspect of reality, combined with the outer or larger universe, is what Einstein might refer to as "General Relative Infinity."

Hauntings and generations belong to the human experience in how human entanglements manifest. One may Google the overlapping connection of quantum physics studies with paranormal psychic experiments to get a sense of possibilities in esoteric physics phenomena.

The PBS network's 1-9-19, Nova documentary, *Einstein's Quantum Riddle*, also seemed to haunt me. That night I dreamed of Guy's visit to Susan and I in a beautiful house before she died on Saturday morning, Jan. 12th. I watched the film, noted some ideas and alluded to them in *Haunted Generation*, line 1: "If seeing it changes it, when is it real?" The rhetorical question answers itself: at each moving change or level "it" is real. The origin of my experience with Susan developed in tangents only to return to the mysterious relationship.

The difference in reading poems verses essays is how poetics assist in creative imagination's more diverse experience. Poems may require several readings to develop deeper imaginative elements with aspects that differ from essays, thus we have "poetic license." Though poems may trigger emotion, it may sound like flattery to express love or like for this or that.

Reading with anxiety acceptance can achieve rich diverse imaginative poetic experience. Anxiety of influence, Dr. Harold Bloom's "diagnosis" in his book of that name, relates to a struggle in a poet's work with a previous poet's work influencing the current poet, as in arrangements of words, what was created by the other, in a way that is contended with, compared to, or composed achieving measures of misreading and internal conflict.

One's Negative Capability may start with ambivalence to nailing down assumptions of what a thing is. One may feel imagination grow in time, get to know it as "it" gets to know oneself (in a form of "entanglement"). This is revealed in dramatic monologues and soliloquies of Shakespeare, Hamlet's conflicted "self-inquiries" or Robert Browning's *My Last Duchess*.

Begin reading with ambivalence to ambiguity. With generous spirit "it" prompts open mindedness to creative thinking, which seems to give "powers that be" trepidation or anxiety for loss of their influence (unless one is well known or desired for a purpose or style). Keats may have had "it" in mind forming *Endymion*, to him, a beautiful allowable failure. "It" can be more democratic, not just subject to the "tyranny" of form, nor one-sided, literal or word by word in declension, but with liberty "found" in limits of form. Paradoxically "it" can promote transcendent processes (before reading Whitman's poems, Emerson knew this in his essays). When approached for fullness of experience of a good poem, "it," can manifest possessing the effect of music, notes in relation to one another, in relation to space and time, the space-time fabric plus god-like "simplification intensity" (Yeats, *A Vision*, phase 17) as in E=MC squared. With abstract art, what one perceives or gets from "it" is relative to what one brings to "it." Musical experience lies with the reader as with the piece.

The experience of the poem's speaker is generalized, specific to one then two people, then to a larger group, then students, as implied to an audience. Readers of the poem, may tie-up to opening observations, questions of the poem's two physics related ideas in a single thought/experience, may share duality of quantum physics principles which: 1. determine actual observation of quantum matter changes "it," 2. "broken in a throw of quantum dice" alludes to Einstein saying "God does not play dice with the universe" as being relative to law and the question of randomness in the universe and quantum mechanics. Implied is "proof of divine grand design" throughout the macro/micro (human parallel metaphor of inner/outer) universe. Among nature's mathematical laws, the firmament stars (and microscopic cellular structures) are God's bulwark for believers against ignorance and obstinate doubt of the divine.

It appears that the grand design part was not enough for Stephen Hawking to accept the divine part. Did his physical condition have some influence on his decision? Einstein appears to have gotten stuck mistakenly about certain over-arching aspects of quantum mechanics, according to the film *Einstein's Quantum Riddle*, (due to mere miscalculations of an equation?). He did not have a problem with the "God playing dice" thought/joke, was this because numbers proved "He" simply didn't play dice with the universe? Aspects of the quantum question are applied to relationships in the poem when assessing what is left of us after our dust returns and dreams have fled.

One need not understand all these things to appreciate poems. They may sound rhythmically intriguing, metrically with musical "numerical shapes" of word-sounds and lines to challenge, mysteriously delight. Poetic ideas may develop from particles relative to people and share some nature of entanglement. People take on time's numerical shapes, on larger but related scales to particles, implied by the "everything is connected" cliché, which both Einstein and Hawking were interested in proving. They conceptualized and failed beautifully to validate with equations, a "Theory of Everything," as the grand unifying principle of the known universe. Duality in quantum relationships, or entanglement, has bearing on an entity in how it effects and is effected by the other, regardless how far apart, or close, as "right there" in perpetuity. Even God for each person had to reduce the law to duality with a caveat. A poem's juxtapositions force the "unity" experience.

"Bell's Theorem" stipulates that particles once having interacted retain some strange link of connectivity no matter how arbitrarily far apart they get. Quantum Entanglement espouses that particles appear to communicate with each other across great distances. The symmetrical nature of the experience has to do with aspects of the universe studied, conjectured and theorized. Everything from shapes of bodies, planets, cells, etc., to the mind of God, seems born out by numerological aspects of the physical universe and time. This mystery may "add up," with specific details, to faith in an unseen greater beyond from this realm to ease the shock and awe of the unknown made known..

Questions arise, arriving at her neighbor's house, with no idea she is the neighbor's neighbor, from over a thousand miles away. More amazing details, after losing track of her again in 1974, involve marriage with her 22 years later in 1996. Susan's last name, always struck me as a combined German/English word, "aus," and "tell." For years that has been what I do with writing and when we married I felt that changing my name to hers would be more fitting, but we did not change names.

In one regard, later Susan tried to defeat me on many levels, while in earlier times she sought to encourage me in those same areas. She became an ultimate human relationship paradox, a true riddle only solved in death. She turned into my sphinx, and the answer to Susan's riddle, being my own man after her rejection, resulted in her slower yet just as real self-demise, done in by her own actions or lack of action, that played out against my best efforts to help her, without being over-bearing or covetous. She won in the end by beating herself, yet thanked me. I will wonder at length what could have changed the outcome.

The only solace, yet the greatest is, the "afterlife" (terrible expression) is far superior to this life, and the dream she appeared in after death, along with the dreams of Henry (dad) and Guy, prove it. This awareness leads to the idea of the true "double jeopardy" duality, the "second death" controlled by God is the true one to fear and we are in good hands there.

Quantum mechanics rings as true as being in the same class for four years of high school with Susan in Germany, because of WWII (the war that caused my birth in Würzburg, Germany) then scattered to different places in the United States, bumping into each other at White Sands, that strange missile base in New Mexico, near the atom bomb test site, (that helped end world war by threatening the whole world) then losing track of each other again only to marry years later …entanglement indeed!

"Years later… late again" …connotations not direct meaning, a feeling more than meaning, yet a truth to tell that infers her last name. These are devises that Shakespeare used and one would be hard pressed to glean a literal meaning from his Sonnets. There are veiled references, allusions, poetic tricks of tongue, compressed time, many openings for conjecture and also personal experience with aesthetic values, qualities, letting the form play into the experience. These aspects make it poetry not essay writing (where the two can and should blend from time to time as they do here). Essays strive for literal meaning qualities and can prove to be manifestos of parsing, poetry is more like a bird one needs to set free to more fully feel experience, hopefully even relish liberty taking flight from its cage of words, in an ironic paradox, to escape when caught (change when seen like photons).

"Remotely sworn" is an allusion to the explorations of quantum physicists into what is termed "Remote Viewing." If one looks up remote, one finds "remote controls" or "far away," viewing looked up finds "observing" or "looking at." If Remote Viewing is searched for, a psychic exercise is found that some physicists have experimented on with the C.I.A. …the point is literal meaning does not automatically usher in the deepest experience with the best poetry, though it can help lay groundwork necessary for a transcendent experience.

A good read of good poetry achieves that thing referred to as reading between the lines, or what is not there, as with what is on the line and how words progress through the body of the poem. The last two lines are ending couplets in what developed as an adapted 3 sonnet "epiphany crown." The three part poem came from a dream series, dreams arriving in a thematic returning or haunting way. How dreams inspired other poems relates to how the first *Haunted Generation* poem occurred after a "mother conflict dream" Dr. Freud would have enjoyed interpreting. Though imagination seemed to play a larger part in the longer *Haunted Generation 2* than in the first poem of that name, a lot came from dream transcription of what happened in both. Form variations turn the three ending couplets into a coda where interpretations are not just for Dr. Freud.

The risk challenge of allusions brought another layer of imagination to the poems. The courage to form the poem is one purpose of enlightenment, as well as stimulation to read and risk open-minded non-judgmental, unconditional positive regard. Negative Capability, ironically named, is essential for this and writing like a true "quatrain meta-physicist" can at times recall Nostradamus.

An exploding supernova of poetry, Walt Whitman adorns the "Kosmos" as he calls it, with his own "silver face" on our poetic language. This silver image of Lincoln is in "When Lilacs Last in the Dooryard Bloomed" (pt. XVI. 197). Dr. Harold Bloom considers it the greatest single poem to date in any language in the Western Hemisphere (A/I p. 237). Whitman's "Lilacs" is the conversation of the "Oversoul's" intimate human song in its true sublime eloquent splendor. Yet Walt was slighted by perhaps the greatest political tactician of modern poetry, W. B. Yeats, in the cosmic, at turns veiled-fascistic, systematically structured judgment of his book, *A Vision*. Dr. Bloom in 2011's *The Anatomy of Influence* (p. 237) points out Yeats' compact judgment on the "Will," of Walt's entirety, voice/persona, as lost in the "Phase 6" paradigm of *A Vision*, where the "soul's free will suffers" another "A. I." –"Artificial Individuality." Here Yeats underestimates Walt's tallied up half-formed consciousness as having "created an Image of vague, half-civilized man, all his thought and impulse a product of democratic bonhomie."

I wonder what the AI of "Alexa" would portend from Yeats' neatly categorized lapsed "one-shot" "judgment," in accordance with an Amazon "Echo's one-shot" (Wired p. 63) "oracular answer?" As of yet "Alexa" cannot write a conscious haiku, much less a quatrain though it could probably beat Bobby Fischer at chess, one move at a time? Yeats may have used a relevant word, "democratic," that has something of a universal aspect appealing to the hope of humanity, in relation to Walt's transcendental "Kosmos."

This leads back to the touchstone dream series that continues: about a month after death, Susan appeared perfectly in her glory, yet unobtrusively, gently, kindly with her utmost beauty's countenance of unconditional love, dutifully standing by a counter of what now seemed to be a "Kosmic" library, in a sublime nature setting, wearing a form fitting sleeveless warm black dress, intricate designs on the torso woven of geometric "curvism's symbolic truthmanship," emerging in chiaroscuro subtlety from the close-up background of smooth flat fabric, more futurist than Moorish patterns but a design subsuming both ideals. Her refined form, more real than her disease ravaged body or William Blake's sublime, rested in resurrected perfection's contentment. Her direct gaze as I slowly zoomed in on her face, perfect form and bettered Mona Lisa smile, stood in service before a fine narrow home bookcase, the top of which could not be seen, as if ever rising. Packed with books on each shelf, spines together, a multitude of color and design fragment like a patchwork mosaic seemed so abstract at first as to be unrecognizable as books, a symbolic web-mystery of life.

Just as Walt's "Lilacs" written for Lincoln, it seemed to also be true for Susan, you or me. I followed a reading of "Lilacs" in the gray solitude of an early April Saturday morning to write an ending quatrain for Walt, Susan, Guy and you:

> Between the lines' material, chasing the moon
> his Kosmos calls for an orbital lilac tree,
> its taproot tallying the orbs of destiny
> as I lie in glowing fields, dream up his night's tune.

To be courageous one confronts fears and lies. There is a saying that good fiction is a lie that tells the truth. When good poetry does this it does so to reach a higher truth than the literal words. There is a certain entanglement on the quantum level of words for dreams and experiences that have a haunting quality. Imagine a quantum physicist approaching the Bible's *Book of Daniel* with a certain clinging quality of dreams found there. They can renew ones spirit and wonder in order to overcome fear of being misunderstood. That process can exert a strong influence to anxiously read and write from, to find if ones words can prove worthy of the love it took to achieve them through fields of dreams.

Acknowledgments

Grateful acknowledgment is made to the following publications, where the poems listed first appeared, in different versions and titles:

University of New Orleans, Ellipsis journal:
  To Helgoland and Back
  Multiple Places on the Lost Highway
  Touching on Rowena's Return

Portals Press, Maple Leaf Rag Anthologies:
  La Belle Orleanna of the Wetlands
  Resurrection Epiphany
  Yeats' Last Paradigm Vision
  Her Unburdened Prescience

Note on quote in Lunar Teacher Eclipse
two lines are from Cynthia Hogue's poem,
Walking the Wasteland in Thule:
"…incarnadined through smoke
the full moon watched with you."

www.ingramcontent.com/pod-product-compliance
Lightning Source LLC
Chambersburg PA
CBHW071353170626
46811CB00003B/1115